Wolve

What your mamma didn't tell you... and your friends don't
know

A dating survival kit

Sherrich Monsher

Wolves in Suits: Dating Survival Kit

Sherrich Monsher

You can visit my website at www.sherrichmonsher.com.

Printed in the United States of America

First Printing: February 2016

www.lulu.com

ISBN- 978-1-329-89927-8

Acknowledgements

Firstly, I want to thank God, who allowed me to write this in the midst of getting a PhD; transitioning into a new role at my full-time job and all the other things that life has thrown at me in the last couple of years. God kept me and helped me to make my vision even more clear.

Secondly, I want to thank every relationship and every date I have been on which helped me to see the true colors of men and their intentions; good or bad.

I want to give a warm hearted thanks to my parents, friends and to my true love (Beastie) that continue to support me, no matter how farfetched my ideas are.

Last, but not the least, this book is in loving memory of Candace McGriff. Candace we love you and miss you!

Anything is possible!

Disclaimer

Let me start by saying that this is not a man-bashing book. There are several wonderful men out there; men that don't cheat, men that listen, men that complete all "honey do" items without complaint. This is just a Public Service Announcement, if you will, to educate my readers about the calibers of men that exist—from the great guys to the horribly bad guys we are sometimes drawn to. Just as women, men go through stages and please know that the men you meet, or even your current partner, may exude some qualities discussed in multiple chapters.

Please Note- Some of the Wolves in Suits stories are loosely based on my actual experiences, while others are stories shared by my tribe (following of awesome women).

Contents

Introduction

The purpose of this book is to enlighten and inform ladies about the well dressed men out there with agendas and schemes. The landscape has changed. Back in the day you could spot a wolf from a mile away. Now, these men look good, are educated, take their moms to church, and get pedicures. They are harder to read and even harder to trust. Seeing them in their tailored wolf suits while facing societal pressures to marry and conceive by a certain age, makes women act before they think and end up hurt, lonely, broke, and sometimes dead.

Some women are in denial and have convinced themselves that they don't need a man; they preoccupy themselves with trying to get to the next level in their company. They have a wall up that was built from fear, horrible past experiences, insecurities, and over all baggage. We can lie to ourselves and say that our goal in life is to be the top at our company or make tons of money—but when you are in your cold bed at night watching *Power*—you have to admit to yourself that you sometimes look over and wish you had a man.

Some silently feel like a failure because they are 27, 32, or 45, and they've either had several failed relationships or have yet to get married and conceive. If this is you, keep reading. If this is not you, keep reading.

I want this book to be as honest as possible relaying what we go through because you won't get what you want until you stop being in denial, and you won't stop being in denial until you see the dating game for what it really is. To you I will say this: there are opportunities out there to meet great men and techniques to dodge the horrible ones, but first you have to be ready mentally. Get out of denial, forgive yourself, and move on from past situations.

We must remember that we are the prize, and the ebbs and flows of relationships go through us. Often times we are so excited that things are going well that we miss and ignore the signs. These signs are critical in defining your present relationship and future interactions with potential suitors.

I have been in a committed relationship for close to two years with a man whom I fully intend to marry; but, for the past twelve plus years, I had been a serial dater. I jumped in and out of relationships like double-dutch, not fully healing before jumping into another wolf's arms. I know their angles, thought processes and intentions. My motto was "what do I have to lose?" I liked them and they liked me, and things seemed to be going well. I was living in the moment more than I was planning for my future or sticking to my standards of what type of man I really wanted. I didn't have a type, and although I had standards, they fluctuated depending on how I felt about the guy at the time. The adage *if you don't stand for anything you will fall for everything* is right. I spent much of my youth falling in and falling out of love; each time causing damage to my psyche, confidence, and view on men. I wish I had this book back then! I would have been smarter and wouldn't have given so much of my love, generosity and spark to men who didn't deserve it.

Before opening this book, your dating decisions were based on what *men* had to offer, as if *they* were the prize. Instead I offer a more common sense approach. Women must educate themselves on the dating scene of today while working to give themselves the same amount (or more) attention than they do to their mates. I know sometimes it's hard to admit shortcomings, but while reading these chapters, you will have an aha moment and you will realize all things you have been doing right and wrong with these new age men.

Now you must realize that this is a new era. This is an era of big fake asses, boobs, and other cosmetic surgery "enhancements". We live in a world where so many women look like models that you may feel like you don't match up. Well you don't have to compete with anyone; you have so much awesomeness inside you. Men do not wake up wonderful; it is a journey, much like the journey you may have been on, or perhaps are still on. Now is the time when you should believe it. It's the time when you should be honest with yourself about what you need to work on. Educate yourself on these wolves. And then, go get your man!

I wrote this book for the old me and the future you. I want you to quit making the same dumb mistakes so you can get what you deserve. I know it sounds crass, but your philosophies have not been working. It's time to try something new!

Basics Glossary

<u>Friend</u>- strictly platonic- you have never been intimate nor has it ever crossed your mind. If it has crossed your mind, you have never acted on it. These interactions are rare, but real nonetheless.

<u>Friend with benefits</u>- *exceptionally* cool friends- you may hang out and confide in each other, but you also screw each other every now and again. You call him when you are sad, vulnerable, and lonely, and he will watch *The Notebook* with you before screwing your brains out.

<u>Boo Thang /situationship</u>- heartbreak waiting to happen- This is strictly sex for one party, but relationship feelings exist for the other person. There may be a specific reason you are not officially boyfriend and girlfriend or dating. It could be because you are the other woman, the man is in transition, or he gives you the old tired line that he is not ready for a relationship.

Dating- the ideal first step- you are going out regularly in public. You have conversations frequently and are in the process of trying to get to know each other. You may or may not be the only person this man is dating and vice versa.

Boyfriend/Girlfriend- you are official- your names are linked on Facebook; you have met his friends, coworkers, and maybe even family. You have pictures together on Instagram and may be each other's #MCM and #WCW. You two are working towards a long term relationship.

Severance pops- that final hoorah! - The final smash down, sex escapade you have before you cut ties with someone. Often time a severance pop occurs after a final break up or right before the final walk down the aisle.

Temperature Check- initial communication- call, text, snap chat, or any form of communication where the purpose is to feel you out and test your mindset. Typically the correspondence will say, "Just wanted to check you", or "I see you doing big things and just wanted to say hello," sometimes, "Hey stranger," or maybe even, "Hey how are you?, How's your work, family, and school?"

Vitamin D- DICK

Australian Kiss- A form of oral sex when a guy goes down on you with lots of sucking, kissing, and licking

Sig- Significant Other

Serial Dater- This is when you jump in another relationship before fully getting over the previous. You jump in another man's (or woman's) arms because you are sure that the problem was them and not you because you are in fact "ready for love". You spend the first 3-6 months comparing your new love interest with your old in an effort to prove to yourself and your friends that you do not miss your ex and you made the right choice by moving on.

Caution- Red Flags you may notice

So what? - The problem with the situation

Sher's Suggestions- My advice, "I'm Sher and give my suggestions☺."

WIS Love Story- Wolves in Suits Love Story

Now let's take a look at the Different types of wolves

Wolf- A wolf is a man that appears to be everything you want in a mate. When you first meet, you are introduced to his representative that is charismatic, charming, emotionally stable, attractive, respectful, educated, makes a decent living, and adores you. In reality this man has inner traits that you would run from; if you knew the truth. Put simply, a wolf is a bad guy in a man's suit and his intentions for you are not pure.

That 'New New'- The rebound relationship; Men are so relieved that you do not have the drama that Dana had or go through his phone like Tammy did. After 3 months this newness fades and this wolf realizes that you were just a distraction from the pain he felt over the loss of his last relationship. (The 'New New' describes male and female behaviors. See chapter 2).

Resume Men- Men who society would say are perfect suitors. They believe they are God's gift to women because of their educational achievements, high salary, and "great sex."

The Dreamer- This man has an aspiration besides having a 9-5 job; he may aspire to be a business owner, author, artist, or even athlete. You are a mistress to his dreams because anything dealing with his dream comes first.

The Newborn- This man is new to being in an exclusive relationship. He could be one of two types: either he has a hard time with commitment and is indecisive on anything that symbolizes a future with you two together, or he has the best intentions, but due to lack of experience he does dumb shit. The latter means well; he wants to do right by you but is learning as he goes. The former, you should not waste your time with.

Sweeper- A wolf whose money, charisma, and looks sweep you off your feet. This man may adorn you with expensive gifts, quality time, and romantic getaways. He prides himself on spontaneity and giving you everything your heart desires.

Homeboy (Wannabe) Lover Friend- A homeboy or good friend who has always been lingering around but you have never dated or slept with. This man adores you, and for years, you have ignored his advances while you continue to pursue other guys.

Bottom Feeder- Moocher, leech, any man who is living off of his woman and controls her with great sex and empty dreams and promises. This type of man wants to screw you out of all your money, time, talents, and energies.

Earthquake Shawty- This man is everywhere and nowhere all at the same time. These types of wolves are trying to get out of a relationship, separated from their spouse, or having trouble securing a job or a home. They have a shaky situation that leaks into every aspect of their life.

Renaissance Man- This man is knowledgeable about everything from politics to the latest rap beef. He is cultured, poised, and classy.

Social Climbers- This wolf's main goal is to have you on their arm so that they can climb the social ladder. This man may be a promoter or have a flashy gig which requires him to be everywhere at all times; and have some hot eye candy on his arms.

First 48- This wolf is the deadliest of them all. This man is strategic, controlling and has the capacity to be violent. He has enough charisma to charm and trick your friends that he is a good guy. When angered, he has a rage so intense that he could very well snap and take your life.

The basics every man should have:

Car: A drivable vehicle- not something "in the shop"

Place to Live: Your mate or potential should have a roof over his head, a place he can call his own. This can be a residence that he owns or rents, just so long as it's not his homeboy's spot or his mom's place.

Job: He goes to work and gets paid- not "they call me when they need me", "I start sometime soon", "I am still in training", or "I have a gig here and there".

Basic Respect- He believes in meeting you at the door, opening your door, and speaking to you and treating you with the utmost respect.

Priorities- He should be trusted to make decisions financially, professionally, and at the same time spending his fruitful time with you.

Chapter 1

The Basics

Some men are good; some are not- but the majority of men have some common "man" traits that women need to be aware of. I would venture to say that half the men don't mean any harm with their behaviors while the other half are trying to use our kindness for weakness. This chapter will help you identify some common male behaviors. Whether intentional or unintentional, if this behavior goes unchecked, you could create a monster or enable an existing wolf. In addition, included in this chapter, are basic attributes that you should bring to the table to keep the relationship exciting and fun! Sometimes we get a man and get super comfy. These tips will keep both parties on point and reveal some behaviors that can't be tolerated.

<u>The Things He Does</u>

- **The Blind Eye**- Many men do not turn a blind eye once they get into a relationship. Expect them to still look at Big Booty Judy, and depending on the age and social network activity of your man, expect him to follow these women and to like their scantily clad photos. If you are very insecure, this may be a weekly argument, but it doesn't have to be. Many times our issue is not that we are completely insecure; our issue is that we don't entertain other guys and behave that way and we cannot understand why our man is doing so. My advice is to speak with your man about how his behavior makes you feel. If he understands, says that wasn't his intention, and will be mindful, then go on about your business. However, after you talk to him and get no action, then you may need to take a deeper look into this potential wolf behavior. There is no good reason a man can give you for giving other women attention on social media or otherwise, and neglecting your concerns when you bring them up.

- **The Booty Club**- Another common man behavior is visiting strip clubs with the guys! I personally like strip clubs, and I attend them with my female and male friends. Often times, these all guy visits are primarily for male bonding and secondarily to see naked women shaking what their mammas gave them. Society says that the strip club is a place where men can go to have a "guy's night out" and have the time of their lives; so they go. That doesn't mean they love the strip club or are comparing what they see on the pole to what they have at home.

Contrary to popular belief, a survey done in 2014 by *Esquire* and published in *Glamour Magazine* revealed that 68% of men enjoyed the strip club either little or not at all. Can you believe that?! I can! According to Kassoy (2014), some of the top reasons that men said they didn't like strip clubs were because they are "expensive, uncomfortably intimate and that they represent men at their worst." Now when your man is spending his hard earned cash at these strip clubs every week and is constantly complaining about not having any money to pay his utilities; you may have a problem. In some strip clubs they do more than just dancing; so a discussion needs to be had about the frequency of this behavior.

- **So you say she's just a friend?** This one is simple: old friends are accepted new friends are not. If your man had a friend prior to your relationship, then he can continue the friendship without issue. If this is a new friend he met at work or at his homeboy's house; this is a definite no and she needs to go! These "friends" end up being the side hoes that come to your Super Bowl party, eat your Rotel dip, and do all the nasty things you won't do to your guy when he says he is "working late". You can identify these women because he will bring them up maybe saying, "So and so brought in a cake today." The next comment will be so and so asked about you. Once you hear this, you know that this hussy is trying to feel out your man and your man is too stupid to see. My advice is to ask your man if he minds you having "new friends". This will give him an insight to how it looks when the shoe is on the other foot.

The Things You Should Do

- **Why must I feel like that, why must *he* chase the Cat?!** Never forget that men still love the chase. Sometimes when we get in serious relationships we lose some of "the spice" that attracted our men to us. This "spice" is not just lingerie and quickies in the bathroom- this spice includes some intangibles that women must keep in mind. Make sure you keep yourself up and engage in self care monthly, hell bi-weekly if you can afford it. Make sure you keep that hair bouncin' and behavin'—whether you have kinky coils, flowing extensions, or a press and curl. Keep nails neat and toes polished! Shave your legs, unless, of course, that isn't your thing. Last but not least, make sure your hygiene is on point, so if the mood strikes you will be ready for action!

- **Have (at least) two things you do well**- Maybe you are a freak in the sheets and maybe you can throw down in the kitchen. Maybe you are super supportive and are his confidant. Maybe you can hang with the fellas but also give him space to hang with the homies. Whatever your strengths are, keep those up and work to be a better woman by improving in other areas you are lacking. A relationship is a two person show and you can't expect him to do everything right while you can't cook, only like missionary, and smother him. Help me help you!

- **Require Date Night**- Do not underestimate a weekly date night. This night gives you an opportunity to connect with your man in between all of the chaos of the world. You can do the regular dinner and movie or something different like a

BYOB painting class, a cooking class, putt putt, go-carting or even seeing a live show! The ideas are endless!

- **Spicy Senorita!** To keep the spice; DO NOT be predictable. Every time your mate calls, don't answer right away—every time they text, the same rule applies. If you were going out with your friends, but they call that day wanting to go out, keep the date with your friends. Think about it—they don't flake on their friends for you—so why do you do it? Also, some men like when their mate is "in pocket". This means you are there, where you are supposed to be when you are supposed to be there. Ex: You get off at 5pm, they call you at 5:15 and you are on your way home. Why not switch it up? When they call at 5:15, don't answer; go to a coffee shop or window shopping after work. My point is; switch it up! Not just to stick it to him, but also so you remain interesting to yourself. When your life is boring and predictable, it leaks into your personal, relationship, and sex life. Make him miss you and when he says he misses you, he will really mean it.

- **Unleash your inner lioness!** Men like when women take charge sometimes—not just with a dinner party or Saturday clean up duty—but other things like paying for a meal, surprising them with something awesome, and of course, taking control sexually. Men love surprises and being catered to, just as much as women! Now a word of caution: Don't take the lead all of the time and come off like a dictator or that you are too independent to need a mate. Just take the lead often enough for him to get excited about you and what you are doing. You know what your mate likes, so you can customize this to fit your relationship.

- **Sex toys and more fun!**- Sexually, you can try something new- this doesn't have to be extreme- you can simply purchase a Kama Sutra or attend a toy party and pick up some new bedroom gadgets.

Or, if you are frugal, just light some candles, buy some sultry smelling body oil and give your man a spontaneous rub down. HEAD TO TOE...

The point is a relationship can go one of two ways: either you improving yourself and being a better woman will make him work to be a better man, or no matter what you do or try, you find out that the bottom line is you have a raggedy man who refuses to do right. Knowing the basics about male and female behaviors is a good start to explaining why people do the things they do. Some behaviors will change because you bitch and moan, but other times, it takes knowledge, that can only be gained when people and relationships mature, to make men stop their bull shit and evolve into the person you always knew they would be.

Chapter 2

That 'New New'

Him: My new girl is so chill, nothing like my crazy ex!

Us: Girl, my new guy is nothing like that raggedy David! I found the one! I am off the market!

This Chapter will reveal the 'New New' behavior in yourself, which you need to check, because it is a main contributor to serial dating, or a behavior that a wolf may demonstrate when he is using you as a rebound. Hopefully, your next relationship is better than your last one, but don't let the newness and refreshing experience cloud you from things you don't like or shouldn't condone from your new partner. Often times, our subconscious is comparing our new mate to our old mate.

Men also are rebound daters who truly believe that they are ready to move on. Meanwhile, they are stalking their ex girlfriend's Instagram page and doing regular temperature checks. Here are some tips to identify this rebound behavior, both within you and this type of wolf; avoiding becoming his 'New New'.

When you are looking for a rebound: Many times women screw up a new relationship before it has time to blossom by comparing their new mate to their old deadbeat boyfriend. This behavior demonstrates two things: 1) you are not completely over your ex, and 2) you like the new car smell but have not gone beneath the surface to see if your new purchase is really a good fit. For example, you find yourself saying, "OMG! I love how he washes my car and gets my oil changed." Maybe this was something your ex-mate didn't do. It's not to devalue or take away from what your new mate is doing to knock your socks off, but beware to avoid falling into the mindset of comparing. Sometimes the reason you love what your new mate does so much is not because of the specific action, but because it was the attention and consideration you were missing all along. Before picking up this book, maybe you didn't have standards of how you wanted to be treated, so any courteous gesture a man showed you seemed impressive. This behavior is one reason you are comparing the old to the new instead of valuing and appreciating your new guy for his distinctive qualities.

Your problem: The problem with this is after you get used to new mate doing a wonderful task or treating you a certain way, you will plateau and their actions will become normal and not extraordinary, but quite possibly, they were normal all along. You will know that you are at your plateau when things that your new mate has always done begin to get on your nerves. *Does he always smack like that? Is he playing Call of Duty* again?*!* When you find yourself in this place, catch yourself and reevaluate some things; Are these things you are complaining about deal breakers? If they are not, ask yourself why they annoy you and determine if you moved on to the next mate too soon. It could be possible that this new mate is a rebound; all the feelings about the things he was doing were temporary, and you just don't feel the same about him once they begin to seem normal.

Your 'Red Flags': The honeymoon period is one of the best times in a relationship. That is when they walk through the door and you want to jump their bones, or you never miss a phone call or text from them. It's when you guys are 'super loving' on social media and go to every function together. Enjoy this time. This honeymoon period could last from 1-6 months, and you feel the shift when this time comes to an end. Often times, we mistake this honeymoon period for the real relationship. One of the main red flags is when you get into a comparison game between new boo and your raggedy ex. If you find yourself bragging to your girls that this new guy is everything your ex is not, then you still have some lingering salty feelings. The reality is you like this new guy because he is everything your old guy was not, and your ability to love the whole person is stunted.

When he is looking for a rebound: How long it's been since your guy got out of a relationship will influence his wolf personality traits. There are some standard behaviors that these wolves exemplify—such as amazement, hesitancy, and bashing their ex. The first thing you will notice about this wolf is that he praises you and seems too often to be amazed by your behavior. He thinks that everything you do is so cool, that he likes your style, your chill demeanor, and your drama-free ways. Each of these comments, are compliments for you, but don't be fooled. What this wolf is really saying is that his ex was not stylish, that she was in his business all the time, hard to approach, and drama filled.

Secondly, this wolf may be hesitant to bring you around family and friends. He may give you excuses about availability and scheduling, but the reality of the situation is that his circle is still used to dealing with his ex. Whether they liked the ex or not, she has left an imprint on them and they are not ready to meet you just yet.

Lastly, you may find that this wolf constantly bashes his ex. He will tell you all the things that she never did, such as support him, do nasty things in the bedroom, or wear sexy clothes. Or, he will focus on all of the things she did too much of, like text him constantly, complain about him going to hang with friends, or put her aspirations before him. Regardless, he likes you more for what you do than who you are and you are running the risk of him walking away as soon as he realizes that you are not what he was really seeking.

Wolf in suit Problem: The problem with all of these examples is plain and simple. This man is not over his ex! Maybe they ended the relationship in a heated argument, but there are two things you must know: they are still communicating with their ex and being with you is a temporary solution to fill the void their ex left. As much as they bash their previous love, parts of them are still attached, whether the feelings are intentional or not. As beautiful and non-drama filled as you are, the attachment to his ex may be something that you cannot compete with.

Wolf Red Flags: You can usually identify this type of wolf. He recently got out of a relationship (less than six months ago) and is already back dating. The red flags are heightened if he had a long relationship (longer than a year and a half) with his previous mate, if they have a child together, or even if they lived together. Also, if you are dating a man who has not had many long term relationships, even if he has been out of a relationship for some time and his ex girlfriend's presence may not be obvious in his life or with his circle, expect the comparisons to still be made, possibly frequently. The fact that they have not had many relationships makes everything you do a comparison. They may not say it, but just know that they are matching up the old against the new in their mind. This is not a horrible thing, but you want someone to see you for your wonderful qualities and sparkling personality instead of judging you based on the qualities the previous lady was lacking.

Sher's Suggestions: (women): Knowing your standards, what you expect and what you like and dislike *before* entering into another relationship (or situationship), helps eliminate subconscious comparisons. Once you reach the plateau of the relationship—the time following the honeymoon stage—you find yourself re-evaluating the entire situation. You may have doubts and feel like you made the wrong decision, or you may suddenly realize that everything about your mate starts to get on your nerves. Stop it before it gets to this point—you do this on the front end by allowing the relationship to grow naturally. Allow a man to date you, court you, and during this time get to know him. Take things slow no matter how good they feel. I repeat: Take. Things. Slowly. You will thank me later. I know things feel good and are exciting and he is everything you want, but force yourself to slow up and PAY ATTENTION! Don't let the daydream of Vitamin D cloud your rational judgment about how you feel and what you see. On the other hand, if your new mate has attributes that you prefer and appreciate regardless of the rebound status, then be grateful, and appreciate your prize. One thing about having a bad relationship, or being on the wrong side of a boo thang/situationship, is when you come into contact with a good man, you appreciate him and may be more flexible with his flaws.

Sher's Suggestions (to deal with the wolf): The more you know the more you can determine the mindset of this wolf prior to committing to a relationship. Make sure you ask lots of questions (in a cool conversational way). Create a safe space for him to share and wait for him to spill the beans on his prior love life. Try to get details about his emotions during and post break up. Listen to the facts objectively without putting your own spin and justification on it like we women sometimes do. Try to see if you can accompany him around his friends to see how they react to you. Observe their reactions to you and notice the topics of conversations; what you observe will give you an insight regarding the hold his ex still has on your potential man and his crew. Now, just a warning, the crew may have hated the ex, making you seem like a breath of fresh air, but do not let this determine if he is ready to be in a relationship. All this means is that they hated his ex and you seem to be a wee better than her. Simply, take it slow with this guy. Maybe he likes you but is not yet ready to move forward, even though his actions say he thinks he is.

Sometimes we make the mistake of test driving the car first (sex), and then letting the feelings develop. This method is backwards and always leaves us hurt and confused. Check out this WIS love story.

WIS Love Story: So I met this cutie at the bar; you know the shy type with good hair, light eyes, and a warm smile. He had clean nails and nice shoes. We sparked up a conversation quickly. He complimented me on my outfit and hair and I said to myself, "This is a guy that actually noticed by effort (unlike my fashion-less ex!)." We exchanged Twitter names and started following each other on all social media networks. Of course I searched through his Instagram (went all the way back to the first picture from 232 weeks ago) and did not see one trace of a girlfriend (in the pics or the comments). I felt good that I had met a cool guy I vibed with who appeared to be emotionally available. The next day I woke up and checked out his Twitter feed; he had tweeted "I miss her" while we were at the bar last night. I thought that was strange, but just figured that I had really made an impression on him! I was feeling myself! It had been a long time since I had made an impression like that on anyone; my ex seemed to take me for granted and never expressed how much he enjoyed my presence. Needless to say, this Tweet was refreshing. We spoke later that evening, but I did not bring up the Tweet because I wanted to play it cool as though I had not been trolling through his social media accounts all night. Later that week he asked if he could come over and chill. I said yes and we enjoyed take out and great conversation. I must admit that if Aunt Flo was not in town (checks to make sure my mamma isn't reading), it would have been on and poppin, but instead we settled for kissing and feeling on each other like some high school kids. The next weeks followed—cool hang out type dates, bar hopping, and shows. I really liked this guy's pace! He was not rushing sex, but I wanted it! I admit his behavior was off sometimes. Sometimes I would catch him staring off into space, as if he was day dreaming. He was also super paranoid about leaving his phone around me, and would cancel on our "Netflix and chill" nights at the drop of a dime.

It bothered me that when he got a call he would leave the room or say he was at a friend's house, but I just figured he was a private guy. He would go to the bar with his friends, but he would never invite me, even if it was a non-threatening co-ed situation, yet I justified all of these actions as signs of him moving at a pace that I had by now convinced myself I loved. One Saturday he came over before heading out of town. I thought to myself *I'm going to give him something to remember while he is on his long drive! Hell he might even come back early from his trip to get back up in this!* I couldn't wait to get the party started, so as soon as he came inside I led him upstairs and started undressing (just to make sure he knew what time it was). When I turned around to look into his eyes he looked kind of scared. I just figured he ain't ever hit anything as fine as me! Surprisingly, his shyness dissipated and he pushed me on the bed! I was like yes! It's about to go down! This was the moment I had been waiting for. He started kissing me, slow and soft on my neck and body! He slipped my panties to the side and started massaging my womanhood slowly before delving in to one of the best Australian kisses I've ever had in my life. I was on cloud 9; he knew exactly what to do to get me ready for our special moment. He kissed, sucked, and rubbed for what seemed like an eternity. I like foreplay just like the next girl; however, this foreplay seemed to be taking an especially long time. I was growing impatient. I was ready for some Vitamin D! Finally, he stopped the kisses and looked up at me—I looked down and saw that he was still soft. He sat down on the bed beside me with a lost look on his face. I could tell that something was wrong because I have never had a guy to remain soft after looking at my sexy ass sprawled naked across the bed! He looked at me and said, "I'm so sorry, I just realized that I am still in love with my ex." We took a break, but I know that is where I need to be." I was humiliated, and felt like I had been led on in the sickest of ways. I thought I was spending time with a guy that was emotionally available, but in reality, his ex-girlfriend still had a hold on his heart and his balls!

Chapter 3

Resume Men

SOCIETY'S PERFECT GUY, MBA
http://www.linkedin.com/in/perfectguy

6222 Mansion Ct · Bourgeoisie, GA · societyperfectguy@mail.com · (505) 555-2222

I wouldn't say I am God's gift to women, but what I can say is I am a humble, down to Earth, hardworking man. I don't have any kids, and I pay my bills on time. I am picky, yet if I feel you worthy to be with me, I will pursue you. I'm better than the rest. Just ask my ex.

HOMEOWNER

Homeowner-5 bedroom house   **2010-PRESENT**
"Best guy you will ever meet"

I am an avid church attendee, especially on Easter and Christmas. Parents love me, and I fit in perfectly with various social circles.

- I make good money, probably more than you, but if you move in you have to contribute

NO KIDS
Kidless   **2010-2011**

- Many have tried, but I haven't found a woman worth carrying my seed.

MULTIPLE DEGREES & AFFILIATIONS

Accomplished Graduate   **2005-2012**

- Received my Bachelors in 4 years
- Received my Masters in 2 years
- Working on an additional professional certification
- Member of the best fraternity in the land

GREAT SEX

Best sex you ever had   **18 years of fulfilling fantasies**

Ask any ex on any day for a reference

Personality Traits: Looks good on paper doesn't he? Finished college; in a fraternity; no kids; goes to church; love pets; and not a dork! Wow! Looks like you lucked up!

Take a closer look before you get fully invested. What is his relationship like with his parents and family? His friends? Does he always make a point to list the things on his resume? Like, how good a man he is; how handsome he is; how he has no kids, how there's no baby mamma drama; how he has one or two degrees and owns his own home. This man looks like gold on paper, but you should still ask questions. Maybe he has no kids because he has paid for several abortions. Maybe he only goes to the praise and worship part of church, without staying for the sermon. Maybe he is a jerk to his friends and family. Maybe he isn't who you think he is at all.

So what? If you ignore my advice, you could find yourself heading down the trophy wife/girlfriend road**.** Put simply, a trophy wife is generally a gorgeous woman whose main function in a man's life is to make him look good at events, on social media, and when the guests come over for cocktails and a games of Gestures or Taboo. This woman's opinion is not valued, and once her youth begins to fade, it's fair to say that the man's eyes may begin looking elsewhere. These trophy wives are expected to have their hair in a certain style, nails a certain color, workout regularly, and dress impeccably every day, hour, and minute. The men who have categorized these women as such feel that these are the types of women they deserve because they are the best men society has to offer. Take heed, these women do not have to be smart nor have opinions on their lifestyles or the treatment they receive; their main objective is to be fine and stay fine.

The next problem is settling for bad sex. Ladies! Please respect your sexual essence and don't settle for bad sex. Don't settle for bad sex because he is a good guy. I know, this sounds like a no-brainer. Some of you are staring with big eyes, swearing this isn't you. But let's get to the nitty-gritty, ladies.

Okay. Go in the other room where he can't read over your shoulder. . .

Now, we are ready to talk.

In your past sex/love life (previous sexual conquests, if you will), you have likely encountered the good, bad, and the ugly—the sensual, the quick, and the waste of time. Often times, with resume men, when everything else is in place— house, car, career, physical appearance, religiosity— we settle for some things. Bad or unfulfilling sex is often one of those items. Our rational angel comes onto our shoulder and says things like this:

What is wrong with you?

Is it really that bad?

But he is so nice.

You will teach him. He'll get better.

You're getting older. You need to settle down.

I mean, you've had enough good sex in your life.

Blah, blah, blah, blah, blah! Ladies... I said, LADIES!!! Do not settle for piss poor sex! Once you start to poke holes in that resume, you won't be able to justify staying just because he seems like the ideal guy.

Now, this is for women who appreciate and like sex. If you don't, and you can do without sex, then you may be okay with being a trophy wife and/or giving the goods to a man who doesn't light your fire (or can't keep it lit) down below! Let me break down how this works!

WIS Love Story: I was in a relationship with this guy who had it all. He had a Masters, was working in his field, was a home and dog owner, and made a decent living. We had known each other for years and he was always chasing me. Finally I gave him a chance. We reconnected at a Super Bowl game, and from then on, we started talking on the phone and going on dates to swanky restaurants and museums. I really liked his style; he was polished and had great conversation. We discussed everything from politics, to music, to love. After one month of dating, he asked me to be his girlfriend. We slept together that night and the sex was *ok*. Not the best sex I ever had, but not the worst either. He made weird groaning noises, and his dirty talking sounded like bad porn. I don't like a minute man, but I don't like that endless sex either. By the end of our first sex session I was dry, tired, and hoarse from yelling *oh yea baby right there* in an effort to get him to hurry up and climax. Other than the mediocre sex, the first three months of the relationship were great!

I felt like I hit the jackpot until all the red flags I had been ignoring started to stand out to me. The first thing I noticed was that he would brag about how much he made in comparison to me. I took personal offense to that; maybe it was because I was overly sensitive about not being where I wanted to be professionally, but still, his comments were rude.

Despite his rudeness and growing ego I stayed. At the time I lived with my parents and every day he would bring up living together. I addressed my fears about the house being his house and if he got mad he could put me out and also the fact that I didn't make enough money to contribute to a household in a big way. *Hell that was why I was still living with my parents!* Finally, however, I gave in and moved in. It took three days to move all of my shoes, purses, clothes and hair products to the other side of town. This was an uncomfortable situation for me because I had never shacked up before, but we justified the move with our future plans of marriage. Somehow, I believed that this was the correct next step in our love's journey. Well, shacking up was not all what it was cracked up to be! I found myself cooking every night, and he was expecting sex every other night. It was almost as if the message in the house was: "Hey, you don't make enough to help me with bills, so I expect sex and food at my demand." The sex had gotten worse and even weirder now that he was comfortable asking me to wear kinky outfits and fulfill more outrageous sexual requests. I tried to avoid sex at all times and when we did have sex it consisted of seemingly endless sessions that never resulted in climax for me. It was all him just huffing, puffing, and moaning on top of me with that hairy beer belly grazing back and forth on my smooth skin. Needless to say, I was unhappy, but in my mind I needed to just roll with it because this man is what society deemed as successful and husband material. Half the time I had a "headache" to avoid sex, and that was only when he wasn't making belittling comments that caused an argument big enough for me to get out of having to give it up. For instance, he had appearance requirements that drove me nuts! He tried to make me choose nail colors that only he approved of, hated when I wore extensions, and wanted me to dress like someone from the 50's. After months passed of bad sex, heated below the belt arguments, me not complying with his "appearance standards," and me seeing him for the superficial jerk he was, I discovered he was cheating!!! The nerve! It took me three days to move in, but only thirty minutes to get my stuff out of his house! On paper he seemed like a great guy; however, he ended up being a superficial guy who didn't know himself, didn't know what he wanted, and couldn't appreciate a woman like me.

Caution: Beware of hidden insecurities and red flags. Many men like these have hidden insecurities. They tend to overcompensate in certain areas and truly believe that they are a rarity and God's gift to womankind. One test to see if he is a resume man (besides his continuous bragging) is to observe him when he is pointing out character flaws. Notice if he is attentive to his own. See if he is reflective about his personal flaws, as he reads you a laundry list of yours.

If you do have issues with his behavior, do not bring it up in a heated argument. Wait until you all are relaxed and in a good space, and say, "Babe, you know what I have noticed?" If this conversation turns into an argument and he gets super defensive, drop his ass! He has shown you his character, which is that of a narcissistic asshole—he believes he is perfect and above any criticism. No matter what you say, he is right and you are wrong. If you do not follow my advice, which many of you won't because your relationship feels *safe* and *comfortable*; you will end up being a trophy wife… until you no longer look like a trophy at least.

Caution: Guys that are building their own resumes

Ladies! Beware of men who are building their own resumes, whether it is their professional resumes or relationship resumes. Some guys know they are not ready for the grand finale and know they need some work. These men, like most people, are trying to figure themselves out, reach a certain point of success, or play the field. Regardless of their status or motives, these men are not taking anyone seriously. They are going with the flow, meeting different women, and enjoying their company, whether casually or intimately. The key to knowing if you are a line on the resume or the wife he is seeking is your ability to read how he acts when the topic of becoming exclusive comes up. When you bring up being official and he makes an excuse, or if he does not mention it at all, then it's safe to say that he is not serious about building anything with you. This man is interested in his own needs and desires; he simply wishes to build his own name. If you decide to get involved, you will be a line on the resume and nothing more. Go ahead and start scouting for his replacement.

Sher's Suggestions: Be yourself! Treat dating like an interview. You are trying to make sure that the company is a good fit for you, just like they are trying to see that you are a good fit for it. You don't have to settle for the first man that wants you. Leave yourself options and narrow them down! Sometimes we put all of our eggs in one basket based on superficial things like money, status, or how well he speaks! Some of these standards are stupid, baseless, and keep us blind, alone, and miserable. Unfortunately, when women get a whiff of some good loving, gain that relationship weight, and start making excuses for the shit their spouses put them through, their standards become lower and the things that were normally unacceptable actually become normal.

More of Sher's Suggestions: You are not the exception.

Women, please listen to me when I say the main reason we end up hurt is we think we are the exception. We think we are the most beautiful and the smartest, have the best sex, and are the most successful.

I am not knocking any of you! I am sure you are the cream of the crop, but what you need to realize is that it does not matter to most men. Most men have their own agendas that have nothing to do with how good you are in bed or how well you cook. The agenda of a man is one thing you cannot control, and nothing you have or do will sway you more or less in his favor.

Chapter 4

The Dreamer

These are my personal favorite. (I don't mean this sarcastically). Dreamers have goals that are above average—they endeavor to reach, sometimes unrealistic, goals they set for themselves. They want to do things beyond clocking in Monday through Friday at a nine-to-five; they desire to run for city council, or become an entertainer, athlete, business owner, actor, or author. These guys may or may not make time for a full-time relationship, depending on where they are on their journey to fulfilling their dream. They don't mean to lead you on, but when they find you, they know they have something good, and they do not want to let go. The problem is you are, and will always be, the side chick to his dream.

Let me say it again. You are a *side chick* to his dream. He will spend time with you *when he can*. The rest of the time, he will be studying, in the studio, or in the gym working toward his goal(s).

Personality Traits: Dreamers either have all of their time and attention focused on one thing, or they believe they are a jack of all trades and display a range of interests. Dreamers also are in their own worlds and have their own sense of time and space. They may not be as considerate as you would expect when it comes to letting you know their whereabouts. They often "lose track of time" while they get lost in their own creativity. Dreamers prioritize their time and life goals by their dreams and what they have determined is needed to fulfill those dreams. If it doesn't contribute to their dream, they refer to it as a distraction— unfortunately, you will likely fall into that category as well.

The exceptions to this rule are dreamers whose dreams include a wife and a family. This dreamer may have aspirations to be principal, or the President of the United States, but a part of his dream includes a family to share in his success. In this scenario, you are in luck! And, you are in an even better position if his dreams line up with yours or are compatible with your aspirations. There is no secret method to finding out these details. A man with a dream wants to tell everyone, unless his dream involves some secret invention. His dream will be a major part of him— everything he speaks and everything he does.

So what? Dreamers need love too! Especially love from a patient, fine woman like you. Dreamers are willing to take whatever you give them. They will not commit to a relationship because it's a distraction and will take time away from them shooting at the gym, getting in studio time, or promoting a new event at a club in town. Dreamers will only make time for what they see as worthy of their time, and you should not expect any more attention than what they give you. These individuals are not looking for a marriage in the suburbs. They want to create their own path with minimum resistance. Let me tell you what happened to me!

WIS Love story: So I was single and on the scene! I had on my sexy stilettos, calf muscles popping, breasts overflowing my top, and abs popping like I was promoting a work out video! I was feeling myself and ready for the world. The night I'm going to tell you about was my first night really getting back out there and I was ready! I was not desperate, but if a guy came at me correctly and had decent looks I would have possibly given him a chance. My girls decided to party in Midtown, which is known for eccentric fashion, crazy characters, and underground music. We found a place where the music was blaring so loudly you could hear it from the street. We went in and straight to the bar. After grabbing an overpriced lemon drop I began to scope the dance floor. The DJ was playing all the underground music I loved and I was letting the rhythms and beats lure me into a zone. The DJ stopped the music for a second and said, "This next one is true underground." When that beat dropped I started swaying side to side to the beat with my designer clutch under my arm and my eyes closed. This was my damn song! I opened up my eyes for a moment and saw a guy standing against the wall staring at me. I can tell he liked what he saw by the smirk on his face and the way his eyes bore a hole in my chest. After looking more closely, I realized that I recognized him from Instagram, @BIGthingssmallpackages. He was some random eye candy I had allowed to follow me and here he was in the flesh. My friend walked up with her drink and we started talking about the music and the selection of guys in the building. @BIGthingssmallpackages approached, and before I could say anything, my friend said, "Hey, Sean!" Apparently my friend knew him in real life, which was a major plus! I figured I would get the scoop about him later on. He offered to buy me a drink and we struck up a conversation about music. Four drinks and six songs later, I was drunk and sweating my edges out. He asked for my number. I gave it to him. His conversation was kind of boring and he was shorter than I would have liked, but I was being open! Our first phone conversation was boring as hell! He spoke only of himself and went on and on about how he has a job working for some independent company, but the job was commission only. He spoke for an hour about how that was just his daytime job; he had plenty of videography gigs on nights and weekends with a strong clientele. I was bored and would rather do fifty burpees than spend another second on the phone with him. He asked me when we could see each other. Though I suggested dinner, he asked if he could come over to my place to cook. Even though he was an Instagram friend, and my friend knew him, I still didn't trust him in my home. I declined his offer and we agreed to meet somewhere for dinner. I suggested a swanky place near both of our homes that had live music, great wine, and wonderful food. He said he wasn't fond of that place and then suggested...wait for it......CHIPOTLE!!! Are you kidding me?? I love Chipotle just like the next girl, but not for a first date.

But guess who went? This girl! What can I say? I was in the mood for firsts. The night escaped us and Chipotle was closed, so we went to *TGI FRIDAYS*. During the dinner he complained about his family saying that he wasn't good enough for them because he wanted to pursue his dream instead of working a 9-5. He said that his brother was the poster child while he couldn't do anything right. After the therapy session (that I wasn't paid for), we departed. I never answered his calls again or had any interest in another man whose idea for a first date was to take me to Chipotle! *HUH*?! Only in his dreams!

Caution: When you run across a Dreamer you can become inspired by their dream. You may be inspired to support them with kind words or even financially. Be careful about being so wrapped up in his dream that you neglect your own. If you have nothing going for yourself, his dreams will become yours. One of the worst things a woman can do is to take on the dream of a man in an effort to keep him interested and involved. Do you know how many women stuck by their men and neglected their dreams so their men could achieve great things, only to discover that once the dream was attained, the men left them for other women? If both of you have the same dream, then you may have met someone who is your perfect match. Otherwise, support his dream while helping yours, simultaneously. In all situations, focus on your desires, your contributions, and of course, your benefits.

Sher's Suggestions: Find some dreams and goals of your own, and focus on those. Spend time with him on your time and not on his. Define your own dreams and goals before you get involved with any man. If you are already involved, stop reading, sit down quietly, and start mapping. You should always have your own long and short-term goals, deadlines, and an overall strategic plan for the current year. When you have your own goals, you are less impacted when a man says he cannot spend time with you while he is in pursuit of his own aspirations. Value your time by spending your extra time with your dreamer instead of spending your idle time waiting on him to call or come by and see you.

Chapter 5

The Newborn

This type of guy is "new" to being monogamous and being in a serious relationship/ not playing the field. He is easy to identify because when you are sharing info about your past (share at a minimum or not at all) he will not have much to contribute to the conversation. He'll share some isolated incidences or maybe a single heartbreak tale. He will admit that his last real relationship was in undergrad or in his mid-twenties. He will blame this extended bachelorhood on needing time to recover from heartbreak, the pursuit of his dream (see previous chapter), or the fact that he has not yet met "the one" (sound familiar?).

Personality Traits: Newborns make excuses to avoid anything that looks or smells like commitment. They are either in extreme fear of being hurt or know that they are not stable enough to be serious with anyone, so they sell you dreams; however, when you catch on to the dream-selling and want out, they beg you to stay. All the while they know they are not ready for a woman like you. That is the worse part about it! The main difference between this guy and the Dreamer is that a Dreamer will be reluctant to get into a relationship for fear that the relationship will be a distraction, whereas the Newborn may not be able to articulate his basis for not wanting to commit to an actual relationship, so he resolves to play the role of a man who sees you in his future.

So what? This type of guy will treat you like the two of you are dating—boyfriend status—but when you inquire about a relationship, he says he's not ready, he's scared, or that it's not the right time. All the while, he continues to have sex with you and have expectations for you... you guessed it—like he's your man. These men know they are not ready for the love you have to offer, but they are too selfish to let you go. They know they will never run across a woman like you, and they are too fearful of you being "the one that got away," so they keep you intrigued and make you feel like they have a plan for you. All the while, they know the truth: that he has no experience in the relationship field and fulfilling your needs is too much of a challenge for him. He cannot love you how you deserve to be loved.

Caution: Initially for the woman, it seems like an ideal situation for the guy to not have a lot of past exes. But in reality, this may later reveal to be a sign of his inadequacies. The first inadequacy is he will say he's not ready when life throws him curve balls. You must think there is some internal reason why this person never committed in the past. The reason may not always be because he has been around the block. It may stem from fear, commitment issues, or just the simple fact that he doesn't handle real life situations well. Or, it may be due to a mixture of all of these things; in which case you really need to reflect on your position.

Secondly, if you are thinking long term, this person may not be the ideal candidate to lead your household. He has a severe lack of experience with responsibility and compromise. He has either been sheltered from real life relationship situations (because he hasn't had the balls to step up and be a man when it's called for). Oftentimes, he resorts to taking the scared victim role and giving a ton of excuses.

These are things he will not share before or during the relationship, but slowly you will see a pattern of how he deals with world pressures. You will watch his inadequacies spill over into the relationship, resulting in him being comfortable where the relationship is instead of moving forward. He will kick it to you as him wanting to move slowly, meanwhile he is avoiding commitment.

A Newborn is one of the worst kinds of men to date because he is a wolf in a really nice suit. Sometimes he doesn't know it, but other times he knows full well that he isn't ready, yet will continuously play the role and pseudo-commit to you in order to reap the benefits. This pseudo-commitment can last two months or two years, but when you inquire about more or the progress of the relationship, he will always give you excuses, hit you with how he isn't ready, or just completely fall back (as the young folks say). The messed up thing about these guys is that when you come to your senses, decide that enough is enough, and cut them off, they come back either with an extremely nice gesture or a plea to reel you back in. Because you truly love his sorry ass, you fall for it time and time again.

Sher's Suggestions: Give him one chance to step up. *One.* If he does not, then leave for good, not allowing anything to make you return. It will be hard. You will be sad. But, you <u>must</u> do this. If not, you will constantly be chasing this man, and you will get the short end of the stick time and time again.

Mark my words: this type of man is the most dangerous because he is either scared and doesn't know what he wants, or he knows exactly what he wants, which is to have a main chick and side pieces (Yes, that's plural). This could be because he is new to the idea of monogamy or he simply is not interested in sleeping with only one person.

If he doesn't know what he wants, you are left holding the short end of the stick until he figures it out. What if you hold on and he figures out what he wants and it isn't you? The flip side of that is what if he figures out what he does want and it *is* you? Would you want a man who is indecisive like that? It is okay to be indecisive with pizza versus salmon for dinner, but one should not be indecisive about whether or not he wants to be with you and have someone like you in his life.

Don't be a doormat, defined as a pathetic desperate person waiting for someone to decide they want them. You are worth more than that. You run this damn world! Act like it!

WIS Love Story: Two years and counting. Two years of wondering if one day he would look at me like I was the only girl he wanted and ask me to be his girlfriend. I had been wasting time in this situationship! I had been acting, supporting, and screwing him like he was my man. He reciprocated the behavior, yet when I inquire about where we were going, he clammed up. His reasons were always eloquently delivered, yet I always walked away confused. The conversation usually ended with me feeling disappointed and stupid. I would threaten to walk away, and sometimes I actually did. Immediately after I'd end it, I'd feel strong, but I'd eventually find myself sad because I missed him. I told myself, "He gets me, accepts my quirks, and I love him," and by the end of the week he would show up at my door with my favorite romantic comedy, my favorite Thai take out, and that boyish look in his eyes. I'd question whether or not I came on too strong, and decide that maybe I should give him the time he is asking for. *I mean, Rome wasn't built in one day, and if he didn't care for me why would he be here?* I thought to myself every time. For several months after the two year mark in our relationship, we enjoyed trips and deep conversations about our future, and he even wrote an entire post about me on Facebook detailing how much he adores and loves me! Now, that really assured me that I was his girlfriend. He didn't have to say it, we both knew the truth. Around Thanksgiving I started feeling like he wasn't feeling me. I couldn't put my finger on it but I just felt like he was treating me like one of the guys. Sex decreased tremendously. I would try to surprise him with spontaneous, kinky sex sessions and he would just tell me that he was tired. Tired? I have never seen a man turn down sex unless he was completely turned off or getting it elsewhere. I didn't know how to comprehend his behavior. In a crying fit, I told him that I felt like he didn't like me; he rubbed my back and assured me that wasn't it. Despite his sincere gesture and sensual love making to try to calm me down, I didn't feel calm. I felt like I was losing him. After a month of limited sex, less frequent visits, dates, and phone calls I knew something was up. I prodded and nagged him to talk to me; I wanted him to explain why he had been so distant. His explanation made no sense. He said that he didn't know what was wrong with him, but it was him and not me. *Right!* I knew what his words meant, and the actions from the previous weeks had demonstrated that he wasn't feeling me. Even though I was cool, sweet, and pretty, he didn't see a future with me as his girlfriend.

Friend maybe, home girl probably, but as his future wife, no. I put my big girl panties on, grabbed my feelings, and said goodbye. He begged me to stay, said he just needed some time. Not this time though; he was out of time and I wouldn't give him another opportunity to disappoint and hurt me. I was tired of being his pathetic option instead of his main dish. As luck would have it, three months after our breakup, he was in a relationship with another woman. On Social media he declares her as his #WCW, Woman Crush Wednesday, and his one true love. His comments made me feel like shit, but I will say that I couldn't be happier about my decision to leave. I walked away on my terms with my head held high instead of allowing him to continue to lead me on year after year. I had my integrity, and honestly, that meant more to me than being in any potential relationship with him on his terms.

Chapter 6

The Sweeper

These types of men usually have a great personality— may or may not be super attractive—but they sure know how to make a woman feel special and wanted. These individuals learn you right away. They know what makes you tick and what makes you happy. Then, they execute operation: MAKE HER SMILE.

Personality Traits: These guys can detect a woman who hasn't been to many places or done many things, and they impress you with fancy gifts and extraordinary gestures to make you fall in love with them. From buying your favorite color flowers, to cooking your favorite meals, taking lavish trips, and showing social network love, they do it all. Be alert, ladies! That does not mean outwardly questioning every action and seeking a hidden meaning. Merely observe his interactions with friends, family, and even strangers to see how he treats those around him.

So what? A Sweeper's angle is to make you the priority and show you things you have never seen before. A Sweeper wants to impress you and have you bragging about him to your friends. Once he has you, full heart, mind, and soul, he starts to show his ass. Different Sweepers show their ass in different ways, but they always make up for it by buying you Tiffany bracelets, dinners at five star restaurants, or mini vacations.

You forgive him, and he throws your past in your face by pointing out that, yes, he messes up sometimes, but he is still better than any man you have ever been with, and unlike your past men, he actually loves you. This whole bullshit spill is all about control and distractions. He controls you with lavish gifts and specialty treatment. Sometimes women find themselves in this situation for the entire relationship. They depend on this man for everything, waiting for him to sweep them off their feet. Check out how this little man swept me off my feet!

WIS Love story: It's not the size of the man; it's the motion in the ocean. Whoever said this never dated a man that was less than 5'5. I stepped out of my comfort zone and accepted a date from a pint size lover. He was small in stature but his bank account was huge! A small town girl like me had never even seen a "black card" and was amazed at how money wasn't a factor with this handsome shorty! During the three months that we dated, he took me on more trips than any man had taken me in years of a relationship. I learned quickly though that money couldn't buy personality, and it's often used to cover up some of the most hideous flaws. My new love interest was also heavy in the church. He sang in the choir, was active in every ministry, and had the Pastor on speed dial. Not saying I am a heathen, but that was a little excessive for me. Nevertheless, it wasn't like he was a drug addict, so I figured I could deal with his super churchy behavior. We took what would be our final trip in the cabins where we could be alone and unplugged from the world. I am not going to lie; I wanted to see what little man was working with down there, and besides some Australian kisses from him, I had not been laid in over six months! My body was ready for some luvin'. After a day of bike riding through the nature paths and a wonderful dinner, we showered and got ready for bed. I came to bed naked as did he. He had small hands, but he used those tiny hands to touch every inch of my body so sensually.

He started moving lower with his kisses preparing for an Australian kiss, and I was ready to cum on myself just from the anticipation because I had not been touched in so long. My knees started trembling and I looked him in the eyes and told him I was ready for him. With excitement in his eyes he hopped up and went to his bag for a condom. My body was aching and so ready for this long awaited action. He sat beside me on the bed, looked at me with sad eyes, softly touched my face, and began to speak. He said, "I like you, but what about what we are doing. What would Jesus do?" *What the heck?! What was happening to me?* This was the wrong time to be bringing up religion! I was so turned off from that comment that I just rolled over and went to sleep. He kept trying to talk to me, but there was nothing to say. I just wanted him to take me home. He wasn't talking about Jesus when his face was in it! It was safe to say that he knew that was our last trip. I was over him. He punked out on giving me some Vitamin D, yet he whined and begged for things like kisses and rubs. I was like: *what man begs for a kiss?? No, honey; I like my men to just steal one!* We returned from our trip. I guess he could feel me slipping away and losing interest, so he bought me yet another shiny gift and invited me to a very prestigious event where many local politicians would be in attendance. I told him I would attend and be his arm candy. Shoot all these months of trips and gifts, I could do him a solid and be his arm candy for just one night. Unfortunately, that week I got news that a relative passed and had to leave for the funeral the weekend of the event. I called him to let him know what happened, and how he reacted still stings me to this day! Don't you know that this man had no sympathy for my loss; didn't say "I'm sorry" or "please accept my condolences." He replied, "Seriously? You must think I am dumb! If you didn't want to go just say you didn't want to go." I was taken aback and hurt; I mean even though I was going to ditch him after the event anyway, something like death will usually evoke sympathy—even in the most heartless of men. I bet that jerk felt really stupid when he saw my post on social media and the concerned comments of all my friends. It's funny how a man so deep in Christ would react so ugly because he thought everything was about him! He swept me off my feet with material things, but when it came to substance and compassion, he had nothing to give.

Caution: Sweeper's tactic is distraction via gifts and lavish treatment. These individuals distract you by fulfilling your every want and need in order to cover up their shortcomings. Shortcomings may include lack of education, class, or bedroom skills, or possibly even jealous or possessive behaviors. You will see red flags pop up anytime you act in a way they deem ungrateful or when you reject their advances. For example, this behavior can surface if you decide to keep your girls night out date instead of accompanying him to an impromptu romantic dinner. If you are too tired for sex, the Sweeper may be appalled and thinking to himself that he deserves to have sex with you when he wants because he buys you fancy things and keeps you laced in luxury. After multiple rejections, his once subtle sexual advances can turn into rude statements filled with entitlement. The Sweeper now feels like he owns you because he has purchased your love and affection with Brahmin bags and trips to the Cayman Islands.

Sher's Suggestions: Sweepers know what type of woman you are, your standards, the good, bad, and the ugly, all within a short amount of time. Sometimes women have the tendency to talk a lot about their past to their new flame. I suggest you only share about your past when you are specifically asked. Sharing can do one of two things: either it makes a man feel sorry for what you've been through or demonstrates to a man how far he can push you before you get upset. Not to say all men have bad intentions, but I want to prepare you for the ones that do.

So for now, do not share, if you have already shared, *say no more*! The less your man knows about you, the more he has to learn, and the less likely it is that he can predict your behavior, which means he's less likely to manipulate and control you. Appreciate the nice things a man does, but do not get so caught up in the gifts and attention that you are blind to his shenanigans. Lastly, it helps to have your own money. That way when you want something you are not waiting on him to purchase it for you.

Chapter 7

Homie Lover Friend

Here's where friend zone meets end zone. "We were friends for years, and then one day I saw the light. I looked at him and saw my whole life!" Have you ever heard someone say that?

 Blah! Blah! bullshit!

This situation is common, and we must address it. Your male friends, who you call when Tyrone or Mike has hurt you, lied to you, and betrayed you, have heard of some of your sexual exploits, your deceptive techniques, crazy ways, and vulnerability triggers. This mix sounds like they would be perfect, like they would know exactly how to treat you.

Wrong!

This type of wolf in a suit could either be genuine or cunning. Let's discuss the latter.

The Homie Lover Friend wolf has the capacity to be manipulative and play on your emotions and vulnerabilities. And, guess what the worst part is. You would never suspect them! You will think they are giving you friendly advice or looking out. Chances are, however, if this person has been in your life all the time and didn't spark a fire inside you that made you consider them romantically, then you are settling anyway if you decide to entertain them.

Personality Traits: Homie Lover Friends are very easy to talk to because they are nonjudgmental. You can literally tell them anything... like about that time you slept with two guys in the same day or about how your boyfriend's sex is awful; they just listen attentively. They are down to see any movie, eat any foods, and attend any show as long as it's with you! They absolutely adore you! They adore you until they can't get their way and want to throw your past mistakes at your face. Read what happened to me and you will see why I think twice before I date my homies.

WIS Love Story: You know that movie *Love and Basketball*, where you have a teenage love and then they grow older and think, "Hey, we were young and dumb the first time we tried to be together, so let's try again when we are smart and established." Well, I reconnected with a guy who had been my friend since forever, and surprisingly, we had a deeper connection than just playing video games and hanging out til the street lights came on. Our first couple of "dates" were basketball games and other friendly type hang out situations. He had grown up to be a handsome man and entrepreneur, and he was still a good friend. Since we didn't define our "hangouts," I still treated him like a friend. I would tell him about my ex's and how stupid they were to have lost me, and also the shortcomings I realized I had in relationships. Finally, after about two months of hanging out, we started a relationship. To my surprise, the relationship was not what I thought it was. Because I told him all of my previous relationship history, he would refer to my ex's in certain situations. He would say, "See, when I tell you something you get mad, but when Kevin used to tell you the same shit, you stayed with him and loved his dirty draws!" or, "When I text other girls or hang out it's a problem, but when you were with Steve that was ok with you." He was basically throwing it in my face that I once was naïve and dumb. I wondered how I got into this nightmare, and how someone I called a friend would use my secrets against me to manipulate me. Never again!

So what? Love, you are settling for what is comfortable and safe, and that couldn't be a bigger contradiction. These "friends" know every inch of your psyche, which is not a good thing. Some secrets we must keep in our private arsenal. Through the years, you have given this man the playbook, and that's the equivalent of letting the opposite team read all of your plays and strategize on how to make you perform like a puppet.

Caution: Take heed to their sly comments. These wolves know more of your business than you do; they're like an external hard drive to your life. On the outside, they seem nonjudgmental, but in reality they figure that you have wasted your time with these losers, so why can't they have a piece of the pie? To get the "pie," they will seem vulnerable and discuss their heartaches with you. Their story revolves around women not appreciating them and how they always seem to fall for the ratchet, low class females. Pay attention to their actions after you share your relationship tea. Do they swoop in like a knight in shining armor? Do they suggest very intimate things to cheer you up? If so, his intentions may not be pure. He may be using your time of vulnerability to sneak in your panties like a wolf in the night.

Sher's Suggestions: Stop telling your male friend stories of your previous failed relationships and sexual conquests. We must be mindful of these things because these Homie Lover friends store this information in a section of their brain and use it when needed. On the flip side, be mindful of stories he tells you about his conquests. This friend sharing will tell you about who he is. Overall, be honest with yourself. This man has been around you all the time and you never desired him sexually or as a mate. Don't let a desperate moment of heartache initiate a relationship that you will regret. Keep him in the infamous friend zone and continue preparing yourself for someone romantically compatible with you.

Chapter 8

Bottom Feeder

This chapter title is self-explanatory. The goal for a bottom feeder is to take you for everything you have and use you for your time, talents, and energies. You may meet a bottom feeder at a club or at the grocery store. Warning: Don't be thrown off by the name; bottom feeders can be visually appealing. A bottom feeder can be a dreamer who moonlights as an opportunist. He assesses a woman's net worth and determines how much she is willing to share or spend to be happy or at least have a warm body in the bed at night. No matter how this woman looks or is perceived by others, women who entertain bottom feeders generally have low self-esteem and other internal issues they have not worked out. These women are often nurturers and have vowed that the next time they get a man, no matter what type of man he is, they will keep him at all costs.

Personality Traits: Now let me get real for a minute. Most of the time bottom feeders provide grade A vitamin D. I'm talking wonderful! They could do things your body has never experienced and touch places you never knew existed. Most of the time the sex and the attention are what hook you. You feed into their ploys and cons and spend your time trying to figure out how you can help them. Most bottom feeders do not have a job at all, and they are not looking. They may be receiving some type of government assistance or disability check.

So what? These guys know how to work the system and have been living off people and/or institutions for a long time. They know how to play the game. The most unfortunate situations are when the bottom feeders prey on single mothers who receive assistance from the government. These men thrive because of the misguided message women subconsciously send in these types of situations—that they need men to feel whole and must keep the man they have because no other man would want them. Sometimes these bottom feeders prey on older women or women who have been married and are now divorced and looking for companionship. They fulfill erotic fantasies and use slick words to get into these women's hearts and beds, resulting in these women becoming their personal sex slaves and ATMs. Bottom feeders aren't always easy to identify. Their objective may not be money; their objective could just be to con you as far and as long as they can. Parker was conned by a sexy wolf who wanted to make her the star of his show!

WIS Love Story: I met my out of the box entrepreneur at Walmart. He was selling CDs out of the trunk of his car. Of course I know this sounds crazy, but hey I am a cup is half full kind of girl, so I thought—self-employed! He had mix tapes, original soundtracks, newly released movies, old school movies and adult movies. Everything you could want to watch was in his trunk! Well, we talked and I bought five CDs for $20, and he said he would throw in an extra CD for my number. I love a good deal, so I cashed in—got me a nice slow jam mix and a potential boo.

Not only was he clever and witty, but he was slim, brown skin, bald and grown! I had never really talked to a grown ass man before, so I was excited! He was five years older than me and a sexy charmer. Since I had been with men who were immature, this sexy man was a breath of fresh air. We went out to eat, movies, skating, bowling. You know, *real* dates. He was also romantic and would take me to the river walk for a picnic on the lake. We were going strong for about two months, when one night I went over to "chill" (really to get some Vitamin D). As I came in and got settled, he was already pouring my favorite wine, *Jam Jar*. He had the incense going and soft music in the background. After making small talk, he leaned over to kiss me passionately as he grabbed my breast through my shirt with one hand and trailed his other one down between my legs. He picked me up off the sofa and carried me to his room where there was a king size bed with big fluffy pillows. He laid me down so gently while kissing my neck. I thought to myself, "This is it! Yes, finally a grown man who is not rushing to just *get there*." I could tell he wanted to make me feel good, and I loved that he was ready to take his time doing so. After I reached climax after climax—D*AMN I didn't know I could have so many*—he held me tight and we fell asleep. I woke up and thought *oh Lord let me get out of here*. This is not my man and we have not defined this relationship! I asked to take a shower, so he gave me a towel and directed me towards the bathroom. In the bathroom I noticed everything I needed was there: wonderful smelling soap, shower gel, and even a SHOWER CAP!!!! I was floored!! You live alone; you are bald so why do you need a shower cap?? REALLY!

I showered and came out the bathroom, and of course, he noticed my demeanor had changed. I asked about the shower cap and he said he just likes to have the things that a lady would need. *Mmmmhmmm likely story*!

I saw many red flags. What did I do? *The usual...acted as if they were green, Go BABY Go!*

We continued our physical relationship for months after the shower cap incident. He was so sensual, and I couldn't get enough! My body had not ever been catered to in that way! He would caress me and ask me how it felt. He would position my body so I could get to feel the full effect of his thrusting. We would ensure I was in the center of the bed so I would not fall out. WHEW! Anyway!

More and more I saw that something wasn't adding up with him, I could feel it, but couldn't put my finger on it. The big revelation was one day when we were about to get hot and heavy making our way to the bedroom and he asked me to wait because he had to straighten up. Now his room was usually clean, and I didn't mind a little mess, so I chalked it up to the fact that he wanted me to be comfortable. He summoned me and I sat on the bed while he was finishing up in the bathroom. While I was sitting there ready for action I noticed a Victoria Secret bag on the TV stand. Well, my initial thought was *who the hell is he buying Vicki Secret for*; however, my thoughts were interrupted by the red flashing light coming from the bag. *What the hell!* I peek in the bag and I see a camcorder...a damn camcorder. Hell nah! I didn't sign a consent form, nor did I authorize the use of my images. I looked right at that camcorder and said *GO TO HELL!*

I was so hurt and pissed! All the passionate nights in this bed where he asked to keep the lights on because he loved my body...all the nights of no baby turn this way, or move the cover so I can see you were all for his porn collection! This man was trying to turn me into a video vixen. Super head...! Not me! Not today!

I politely got up, put my pumps on, and walked out the door. He called and texted, but I never responded. I was confused and mad, and no discussion was going to make me feel better. I wasn't sure if this was the first attempt or one of many, but I knew I wanted to get away.

About three months later I saw that fool still outside selling his movies and CDs. I walked up on him and said, "I want the one featuring me and you!" He was floored. He smiled that charming smile and said, "No, my love. That was for my eyes only." *Boy stop*! I was un-amused and unbothered. He gave me the "I never wanted to hurt you... sorry...blah!

blah! Blah! Blah! Bullshit! I walked off as he called my name. I went into the store and never looked back.

Caution: Fortunately for Parker, she had been observant; otherwise, she would have been a porn star minus the porn star income. Observation can help you when your intuition and mind is cloudy from good sex. The good sex bottom feeders distract you with deeply penetrating vitamin D so that you don't notice the obvious and start asking questions.

Another red flag is that this type of man wants all of your time and attention. Bottom feeders frown upon you spending any time and money on any one else but them; this includes yourself and your kids if you have any. When you spend money on anything that does not include them they can behave like a spoiled brat on Christmas. If you think you have a bottom feeder, a good test is to go on a shopping spree. You can spend your money on everyone but him. If he judges you, seems very upset, or calls you selfish and throws a tantrum, take it as a red flag.

Bottom feeders will also make promises to contribute to the household when in reality they have no desire to help out financially. They make promises, telling you they are interviewing and can't find a job, but they *just know* something with come through soon. They ask if in the mean time they can stay with you until they get on their feet. All the while, they hold up in your home running the electricity and watching Netflix! You would think that this was a violation of man law and that this would make the Bottom Feeder feel like less of one. WRONG! They are not wired with the qualities that allow a man to lead a household as a provider.

Sher's Suggestions: Let's get this straight. This woman is not just a helpless victim who has no say in her fate. We have resources like this book and our own common sense to help us out of these types of situations or prevent us from getting into them in the first place. People treat you how you allow them to, and at this point in life, if someone is using you for your money, space, and time, and you are fully aware and don't want to change the situation for fear of losing your man, it's your own damn fault.

You are not a victim! This is not an example of a man! Get your shit together and stop being so desperate for such a wolf that doesn't care for you and uses you for his own benefit. Remember, the difference between any of the other types of men and a Bottom Feeder is that a Bottom Feeder is an opportunist and a con artist in a suit.

Chapter 9

Earthquake Shawty

By the end of this chapter you will be asking yourself:

Am I dating someone who is in transition?

Am I in transition?

What do I do next?

How would you want someone to treat you while you were in transition?

Would you want a friend? A boo or a Relationship?

Keep these questions in mind. If you were in transition, would you be available to develop a relationship while also trying to get on your feet? If the answer is truly no, then consider a friendship instead of a full-fledged relationship. Think of the bright side. If you develop a friendship during this rough patch, by the time the rough patched has passed, you will have created a foundation for a possible lasting relationship. The types of transitional men, I will discuss; are those going through job transitions, divorces, and Mr. Potential.

The Unemployed

Personality Traits: The three main types of job transition situations are a person with no job, a person who is in the process of changing jobs, or a person venturing out on his own to start a business. Let's start with a person who has no job. He may find himself unemployed because of a layoff, termination, or resignation. Either way you cut the cake, he's not clocking in and out of work every day, and even if he has unemployment funds or a severance, his income can be somewhat stifled. The other scenario is a man, who is changing jobs or is taking this opportunity to fulfill a dream of being a business owner. Though each of these men has more potential than the former, the time dedicated to achieving their goals will come at the sacrifice of the time they would have been spending with you.

So what? During this time, the man who is faced with the personal and societal expectation to be the provider may feel less than in many areas. Depending on how long he has been out of work, he may become increasingly irritable and less emotionally available for a relationship. It is during this time a man will begin looking for another job or step out on his own. If he chooses the latter, he may transition into the Dreamer stage. Please see chapter four for a more in depth analysis of this type of guy.

Caution: If a man is in transition due to unemployment, he is most often vulnerable and insecure. He could come off as sensitive to comments and lash out about last minute details or discussions. If society instills in a man that he is a provider, then not being able to provide sends the message that he has failed at his one task. Men may feel this way even if you are super supportive and encouraging. This is a man thing and they won't feel whole until they gain employment. Men who are using this opportunity to take a risk and follow their dreams will become increasingly focused on their goals and less focused on you.

At times, they may even see you as a distraction. Their perception of you may go from an asset to an obstacle holding them back from pursuing their music in New York.

Sher's Suggestions: Here is the key to the guy in a job transition. If you are already in a relationship, by all means, stand by your man. I will warn you, your man may become agitated about not having a means of income, especially if you have children. With the support of a good woman, a man will be able to get a job and he will appreciate that you stood by him through his lower moments.

Here is the flip side to that.

If you, as a single woman, meet a single man and he doesn't have a job, this *will* put a strain on the relationship. You want sushi, but his money is tight, so he can only afford pizza or nothing at all! You may be saying to yourself that this will be okay and you can deal with it. This sounds real cute, but you will often have to pay the tab, and he will always feel like less of a man, or even worse, he will not mind you taking care of all the expenses. It will get old really fast.

If you are hard headed and want to make it work with this potential mate, then help him find work, update his resume, and take him to networking events. If that sounds like too much work, then take the friendship route.

When I say friendship I mean just that. *Keep those legs closed.* I know you don't want to listen, but you bought this book for another perspective, some insight, or some help because what you have been doing has not given you the results you want. You have to do something different to get different results.

The Divorcee

Personality Traits- Sometimes you meet a potential mate who may be going through a divorce. Some of these individuals are actually going through the process of a divorce, some are legally separated, and others just say they are going through the process; they just haven't contacted a divorce lawyer or informed their spouse yet. No matter the circumstance, this man is still married and considered unavailable.

So what? If you are going through a similar situation, this in-between stage may work for you both. If you are single though, you may just want to keep this relationship as a friendship. Keep those legs closed! If you don't, you may become a victim of a rocky marriage fling. Sometimes people intentionally seek out these flames for a quick thrill, and other times they are vulnerable and want to see what else is out there as a distraction from their marriage falling apart. This may sound like a fun fling with no strings, but do not underestimate the potential emotional connection you could have with this person. Sometimes women have been through so much heartache that they take what they consider the "man approach". The man approach is to sleep with whomever you want and not go on any dates, no long phone calls; situationships are founded on text messages and nasty pictures. The only corkscrew in this seemingly ideal arrangement is emotion. Emotions are unpredictable and inconvenient. You could really vibe with this person, yet because you didn't anticipate the connection, you decide to have casual sex, and inevitably, you are caught off guard and totally unprepared when feelings emerge.

Caution: These men are no different than a man with a girlfriend. They are unavailable and have serious baggage. This baggage is ignored while they are making you scream and moan, but it's pending nonetheless. The worst part of this is often times a man is not going to come out and admit that he is getting a divorce. Normally, men say they are separated and don't live in the same house in order to appease you. This may be true, but the fact remains that this is still a married man, legally and morally. Now I am not an angel, but karma is a bitch; just let that thought marinate. You are still only working with half a man, financially and emotionally, if his soon to be ex-wife is busting his balls all the time! This man is all over the place so in reality you may be a rebound; either until he comes to his senses or until he mends things with his wife "for the sake of the kids". Let me tell you what happened to my friend Rosa.

WIS Love story: Who says you can't find love at the club?? I was with my home girl watching the basketball game at our favorite local bar. The drinks were flowing and we were stuffing our faces with wings while scoping out the eye candy. This sexy man and his friend approached us and we ended up talking and laughing all night about everything from sports to music! What a random unexpected double date with two strangers. Me and cutie exchanged numbers and promised we would get together soon. I asked him if he had a girlfriend. He said he didn't, but he was in the process of getting a divorce; he was legally separated at the time. We met for lunch the next day and he told me about his situation and how the divorce should be finalized within a couple of months. From that lunch on we hung out almost every night at my place. One night after a movie we went to his place downtown. I went inside and the house looked so empty. He said his soon-to-be ex-wife had taken all the furniture and moved in with her sister. Even though the divorce was not final yet, this empty house sure proved that he and his wife were done, and that made me feel more secure about his situation. We spent the next three months ordering lots of take out and going to hole in the wall restaurants that had great food, but you would need a tour guide to find. I couldn't shake the feeling that he was hiding or scared of someone. When we would go out, he would always look over his shoulder and he never posed for pictures.

I just chalked it up to the fact that his divorce was not final and he did not want to parade his new girl. Plus, when I asked about the divorce status, he would get testy and we would argue, so I just decided to keep my mouth shut. I mean, other than him wanting to remain anonymous outside the house, he treated me well, gave me great Vitamin D, and paid all my bills. When I say all, I mean utilities, rent, car note, and weekly lunch money. What more could a girl ask for?

One night while we were lying in bed, his phone began to ring. I grabbed it to hand it to him and he yelled at me about touching his phone. The argument turned heated, he grabbed his phone, threw on his clothes, slipped on his shoes, and stormed out. I was so upset! He yelled at me, left, and still hadn't called to apologize. *What was freaking wrong with him?* It was already bad enough that the world didn't know we were together, and now, on top of that, he just leaves like that! Now that I think about it, in the previous couple of weeks, he hadn't been staying the night and when he got home, he never called or texted. I was getting more pissed by the second.

The next day, he texted me about hanging out! Hanging out?? This fool was about to get cursed out! I had not heard from him after we argued and he left, and now he wanted to *hang out*?! Instead of texting, I called him back. He did not answer. *I know he saw me call! What was up with him?*

I was pissed! Why was he ignoring my call when that fool just texted me. My phone rung and it was him. I answered and immediately said, "What the hell man? You come over, screw my brains out, argue, leave, and won't even answer my calls??" There was silence on the line. I thought I left him speechless, but then I heard a female voice say, "What bitch?" *Bitch*? "Who is this and where is Max?" I asked angrily. "This is Max's wife!" the voice yelled, "and you are a hoe who needs to leave other people's man alone." *A Hoe?!?! How dare she call me a hoe?* Did this asshole have his wife answering the phone? I thought they were done; at least that is how he kicked it to me. I was so hurt, pissed, and humiliated. Before I could tell her that I had been told she was out of the picture, she hung up on me.

I was crushed! Not only had he been lying about his situation, but I seemed to just be something he was doing on the side to entertain himself. I don't know what was worse, having a woman you were told was out of the picture call you a bitch, to be sleeping with someone's husband and not know it, or thinking your guy is available when in reality he has an unstable situation and has involved you in the drama.

Sher's Suggestions: How many of you can relate to Rosa's story? First and foremost: know the facts! Find out the real reason why this man is in transition. Being patient and generous, and lending your time, energies, and talents to a person in transition is not a crime; just make sure your deeds are not in vain. If they tell you the scenario, ask questions in a considerate manner, but also ensure you get the answers you need to determine your future with him.

It may be wise to have more of a friendship at this time if the transition is more complicated than you are used to. This person may not be available for a relationship, but a friendship could prove to be valuable for you both. Your heart and your empty cold bed may say you want a relationship, but let your head think for you at this time. If you are also in transition, your focus should be yourself; everything else should be secondary. Now let's look at the last Earthquake Shawty, Mr. Potential.

Mr. Potential

Personality Traits: You may find yourself dating Mr. Potential if you are afraid to give up on a man because you see what he *could* be. You tell yourself he just hasn't gotten there yet. The personality traits of Mr. Potential are the excuses you make, not actual traits the individual displays. The excuses sound like this: once he gets a divorce, he will be less stressed and that will make our situation better; once he gets another job and makes more money, we will be better and he will be more focused on me. Once he gets some therapy, he will be happier and our relationship will be better.

So what? Let me let you in on something, men do not date our potential! Men do not give us the benefit of the doubt. To them, what they see is what they get. They look at us for what we are and what we have to offer at the moment, and then they decide what level they want to put us on—casual sex, boo thang, dating, relationship, or wifey status. It is that simple. Most men like when a woman has things going for herself and is happy and content enough to be available. If you are drowning in misery, in between jobs, and depending on him for finances, do not expect him to stick around, and if he does, he will not be happy and surely will not be faithful. Men can appreciate someone that is on their level. Don't let the media make you feel like housewives who built their wealth on the backs of others are what men desire. A man of good character wants an equal partner, not a gold digger more interested in image and status than building something together. If you want a man that just wants you to keep up an image, then I know a good therapist I could recommend you to.

Caution: Mr. Potential doesn't necessarily know that you are sticking around, until they evolve, but they do know that no matter what they do, you stick around. These guys push your limits by doing regular guy shit that grinds your gears. They have a knack for stringing you along in every scenario by making promises about the future. They may say, "Babe, once I land this head chef position at Ritzy Restaurant, I can leave Taco Bell," or, "If you just hang in there with me, I will give you everything you want and deserve." The *what if* intrigues us and lures us closer to this man. We become too curious and invested to leave. The difference between Mr. Potential and the Dreamer is that the Dreamer is more reactive while Mr. Potential is more proactive. The Dreamer focuses on his goals and makes promises when you're ready to walk out, while Mr. Potential weaves his false promises throughout the entire relationship. Mr. Potential may or may not stick around once he reaches his potential, and hell, that's if he ever reaches his potential! Please note that some men are still trying to get to the next level and have the purest intentions for you. These are not the men I am talking about. I want you to be able to distinguish the men with good intentions from the wolves.

Sher's Suggestions: The one question that should guide your interactions with Mr. Potential is: if he doesn't ever change, would you still want to be with him? If the answer is no and you're a softie, I would suggest you reduce the interaction to a friendship to salvage hope of maintaining some sort of a relationship. If you are strong, can make clear decisions, and want to date someone who is as mentally, financially, and emotionally available as you are, then tell him to kick rocks and proceed on your journey to find your Mr. Right. I do not want you to get the word "available" confused with "someone on the same level as you". He may not make over 50K like you, or have a house as big as yours. He just needs to be emotionally, mentally, and financially AVAILABLE, meaning that he is in a position where he is stable enough to divert his energies from things like work and himself. This individual may want more in time, but for now he is happy enough in life to be able to have a meaningful and healthy connection with someone else.

Chapter 10

Renaissance Man

Have you ever seen the commercial about the most interesting man in the world? The 'Dos Equis Commercials' show us a man who is well versed, mysterious, seasoned, sexy, and someone who all the women want to get close to.

Personality Traits: In a nutshell, Renaissance men know something about everything. They are educated and well versed in poetry, politics, culture, and just life in general. They have characteristics like a sweeper, but sweep you with their conversation and mental stimulation more than their money. Renaissance men are a delight to be around because they open your mind to art and culture, music and wine, gourmet food, and travel. They are not the mainstream, like the rest of the guys who are listening to rap and pop. These men are classy and can mix with the best, but also down to Earth enough for you to introduce to your girl friends.

So what? Their angle, just as the sweeper, is to impress you and hold your attention. These men may not be sexual with you, but if they are, and you all are not in a committed relationship, then they are likely juggling multiple women at one time. If they are not having sex with you, they will keep you mentally entertained with cool dates and out of the box conversations. They will discuss dreams and goals without being judgmental or taking a negative tone towards your thoughts and ideas. On the other hand, they may be another woman's man fling, boyfriend, or even husband. These men have to be stimulated mentally, but they have not found a woman to hold their attention. For this wolf, mental stimulation is a drug. When paired with good sex and some home cooking, you will get a man who will never want to leave. Just be careful that he isn't holding on to you and someone else, or even worse, that he isn't a Renaissance fraud. Let me tell you a quick story-because it happens to the best of us.

WIS Love Story: Girls night out!!! My friends and I looked sexy and were on our way to the new Comedy Club downtown. We arrived, ordered drinks and got some seats that were not so close that we would be the brunt of the comedian's jokes, but not in the nosebleeds either. Next thing we know, one of our friends walks up with a guy! A fine, tall guy might I add! We were bummed! This was our night!!! But, we were nice to the hard leg, and he was charming and just went with the flow. Apparently he wasn't told it was girls only! After the show, we left and the uninvited party pooper man asked could he speak to me. He clarified that he wasn't with our friend, and that they were just friends. He was interested in getting to know me. I gave him my number and we tried to make plans. He wasn't local so we planned to get up later in the summer. He called the next day and asked me to come down to his hometown, which was about an hour away, so we could chill and spend some time together. Even though we were initially going to get together later, I decided go, I mean what did I have to lose? The day was great, he cleaned my messy ass car, grilled for me, and we had great conversation. He was so well rounded and knew everything from sports, crazy reality shows, politics, and food. He was so sincere, with a great work ethic, great values, and a little bit of mystery that gave him a sex appeal that piqued my interest.

I appreciated his work ethic in that he had worked all these years to study and pass the firefighter test and now every day he was risking his life to save those in emergencies! That turned me on, but something told me to save my goodies for the moment. Thank goodness I did!

I told a friend about him who lived in the same city, she said that she was dating a firefighter and would ask him if he knew my new boo. The next day she called me and said, "Girl, he is no firefighter the word on the street is he cannot pass the test and he is the do boy at the fire station." I told her that she didn't know what she was talking about. He gets off the phone with me to fight fires every day, and he even has him shooting the hose on a scary fire as his Facebook profile picture. Even his

Facebook name has the word Firefighter in it! Why would he lie?? But she confirmed that, yes, he was lying, and, no, he was not a firefighter on any day of the week because he could not pass the test. I called that joker so fast and gave him a fiery cursing out! I was so pissed, not because I liked him so much, but because every day he was lying to me about being at work handling fires when in reality he was fetching water for the real heroes? I told his lying self not to ever contact me again. My Renaissance man turned out to be a fake ass, no real job having ass, fraud!

Caution: This type of wolf is always one step ahead of you. He is smart, strategic and has his juggling act to a tee. Sometimes he can come off as pompous, which may trigger some insecurities and make you feel less than. Like the Resume man, this type of wolf knows how to play on a woman's intellectual insecurities. They use this as a defensive mechanism when you begin to question them about their whereabouts or possible secret lives. They have the capacity to degrade you on a higher level using calculated jabs to your self-esteem. In the above WIS love story, this wolf was harder to detect because he seemed sincere. This wolf had mastered living his lie.

Sher's Suggestions: Once again with this wolf, just like all the other suits, make sure you know the facts. I am not saying stalk his Facebook, etc., I am merely instructing you to pay attention to his mannerisms. *Does he always have his phone on silent? Does he look like he will faint if you pass him his phone? Does he only speak to you while in the car or see you only on weekends? Can you call him just about any time of the day and get an answer?* Stay alert with all men, but especially this one because the mental connection you have with him could blind you to the fact that he is hiding something. You would learn much from this man, and IF he is available, this may be a good relationship or friendship for you. However, be cautious because he may be smart and classy, but he also may be hiding something or someone he doesn't want you to discover.

Chapter 11

The Social Climber

You ever been to an event with your significant other or on a date and you were not looking forward to it because you felt like you'd have to babysit? Often this occurs if your date is unfamiliar with the rest of the party or if he's socially awkward. Well, these are not the men I am talking about.

Personality Traits: Social Climbers. They're always on the scene with a gangsta lean! No, really, these men are always on the scene. The scene, means every party, event, and outing Monday through Sunday. Their goal is to be seen and known by all, in every circle. Social Climbers main purpose is to rise to the top whether there interest is politics, entertainment, or Socialite status. These men will do ANYTHING to rise to the top and will not let anyone stand in their way. Their life goal is to be everywhere and be accepted and liked by everyone. They will use their VIP status to get you into the most desired establishments and most highly anticipated shows and events.

So what? He can't keep his butt at home! These men are ideal for women who pride themselves on being arm candy in the spotlight. If you are a homebody, this type of man is not ideal for you. You will soon tire of being out in the streets every night, and the more you opt to stay home and watch Netflix, the more prone he is to view you as a boring prude.

This is the type of man whose desire to rise to the top and be in the public eye is stronger than his desire for loving you. The Social Climber's desire for public attention is the most important thing to him. You, as his lady, are negotiable; if he has to choose between going in on a VIP booth at the grand opening of the hottest new club and attending your family holiday party; he will be sincere when he sends you his well wishes. He will do ANYTHING to keep up appearances including lying, scheming, living beyond his means, and manipulating you and others. There is no love, maybe sex, but no real commitment. If you are in a relationship like this and you love it, then keep up the charade, girlfriend! If not, assess the return on investment and decide if real love and companionship is what you are seeking. If so, dump his ass and use this book to help you get back out there in the dating world, not as a sheep with the wool pulled over its eyes, but as a woman in the know.

Caution: Social media reveals a lot of the red flags for this social climber. Believe me, no matter his age, if he is a true social climber, he is on some type of social media. He is constantly scrolling through social media, subscribes to all of the club email VIP lists, and knows what everyone is doing in the city at all times. For this wolf, being seen and making connections is the priority. Life events that regular people attend like baby showers and class reunions are rated to determine the VIP status of other attendees before they will agree to attend. They will not blatantly turn down your invite; they will just blow you off or say they have a prior commitment. For instance, if an event has minimal exposure, meaning no one the Social Climber deems important is planning to be there, then he will not attend. No matter how much this event matters to you, if he deems the people at the event beneath him, he will not accompany you. Exceptions to this rule may include events for their children, but even that's not a guarantee. Additionally, they spend a lot of money appearing to be on top of their game when they do attend these events. They have an outfit for every occasion and will not duplicate a look for fear that someone may post a picture on social media. This type of wolf isn't keeping up with the Joneses; he is Mr. Jones and believes that he has followers and people who idolize him. These fresh clothes and VIP nights can be taxing to your relationship physically, emotionally, and financially.

Sher's Suggestions: This type of man would be a good option as a guy you put in your dating rotation. You can be his arm candy when you want to get out of the house and visit the up and coming lounges and clubs or even major events. It's hard to give someone 100% of your attention because you end up leaving nothing for yourself, so do not try and keep up with this man. You will tire yourself trying to accompany him everywhere. You must be real with yourself; if you are not a turn up queen, then do not pretend to be. If you feel like you can hang and decide not to take my advice, be prepared. Be prepared to come in no earlier than three o'clock in the morning on the regular, to make up excuses for why you're late to work, to grow accustomed to horrible hangovers from partying, and to spend your quality time with your man and the spotlight. If this type of man and this lifestyle tickles your fancy then go for it. If not, this wolf should just be one of your options for when you're bored or you should leave him alone altogether. The main priority of a social climber is not a relationship, and every interaction, including dating you, is a business deal. This wolf specializes in using people as chess pieces to move through the game of life, and he would accomplish this goal with or without you. Let me tell you about the shit that happened with my homegirl Victoria.

WIS Love story- Fortunately, and unfortunately, my entire life has been spent in the spotlight. My father has been involved with city, county, and state politics for as long as I can remember. While you were playing outside until the streets lights came on, I was participating in pageants and debutante events. My high school life consisted of hanging with the top ten percent of the class, and my future has always been laid out for me, especially my love life. Once I reached adulthood, my family's life came under more scrutiny because my father was running for state government. Although I yearned for adventure, a life like this leaves little time for freedom or youthful, reckless behavior that many reminisce about when reflecting on their younger years. In exchange for having all of the material things a girl could ask for, I had never experienced true love because my path was always predetermined. At last year's Gala, I met a handsome attorney named Bruno from a prestigious family. He approached me with excellent manners, a tailored suit, and beautiful hazel eyes. We spent the entire night talking about ourselves and how we couldn't believe that we met each other at such an uppity function. Before leaving, I introduced my new friend to my father, and he surprisingly seemed to approve. Bruno and I began to see each other regularly, and after two months of dating, we decided to take things to the next level and continue with a committed relationship. Bruno treated me like a queen. He had his own place, his own money, and most importantly, Daddy loved him and trusted him with me. Bruno would work lots of late nights, but would always text or call to tell me he was thinking about me and how he couldn't wait to see me. We had not been intimate because he said he wanted to wait until marriage. Men like this were unheard of! When we were together, there were endless laughs. We talked until we fell asleep, shopped, and just hung out. One thing

Bruno and I had in common was that we loved to pamper ourselves. We would go together to get massages, manicures, pedicures, and even facials. One night, Bruno sent a text that said, "Working late on this case so I won't be home anytime soon so don't wait up. Miss you." *Poor thing*! This was the third night in the row that he had been at work late working on this stupid case. He had to be exhausted, hungry, and under a lot of pressure. I decided to surprise him with food from his favorite vegan restaurant and a pair of Morehouse sweats and a t-shirt so that he could be comfortable for his all-nighter.

When I pulled up to his office, the lights were off and there were only two cars in the parking lot. *That's funny* I thought to myself, *I thought more people would be here.* I entered the building using Bruno's code and made my way up the stairs while trying to balance the vegan lo mien, my purse, and the duffle bag of his clothes. When I reached the top of the stairs, I could see a dim light coming from under the door and could hear some soft music playing. *This is an intimate setting for work on a murder case* I thought to myself. When I opened the door what I saw made me drop the lo mien all over the hardwood floor and clutch my pearls in disbelief. Bruno was on his hands and knees sucking the hell out of a man's dick. The man was enjoying himself and groaning and saying, "Yes, yes suck it with those pretty lips." *What the hell is happening right now?* No wonder he wasn't interested in getting physical with me. Apparently Bruno had not heard me come up the stairs or realized I opened the door. I screamed, "Bruno what the f*&%?! So you like men?! How could you? You son of a bitch! You are licking this guy's balls and you were going to come and kiss me with that mouth!" Bruno, after wiping the deer in headlights fear from his face, said, "No baby wait! Let me explain!" What was crazy is his lover just looked at me with an *oh well bitch* look on his face while his big black dick was just hanging out. I ran down the stairs hurt and vowed to never speak to Bruno's dick sucking ass again! After a night of crying my eyes out, I woke up feeling like shit and looking even worse. I had turned my phone off and when I turned it back on I had seventeen voicemails from Bruno. I did not listen to any of them. Instead, I proceeded to get myself together; I could not be seen on the streets looking like someone off the five o'clock news, so I decided to get myself together before I went to my parents' house to tell them what happened. I called my hair and makeup artist over to the house, and I was looking and feeling like myself again by noon. When I arrived at my parent's house, I saw a car in the driveway I didn't recognize. However, this was common at my parents' house. When I walked into the foyer, I saw Bruno in the sitting area talking to my dad. Bruno saw me, and before I could speak one word, he whisked me in his arms and gave me a kiss with the mouth I had witnessed filled with another man's dick! He held me tight in a warm embrace and whispered, "Say yes. If you say no and my secret comes out, I will bring down your family with me." Before I could process what was going on, Bruno got down on one knee and proposed. I was stuck because I did not want to unravel my family's legacy due to poor judgment on my part. All of the signs were there: the lack of sex, the manicures, the "girl talk," yet I missed it! Six months later, we had a wedding priced comparably with Kanye and Kim Kardashian's. As the pastor asked, do I take this man; I smiled with tears in my eyes and said, "I do." To save my family's name I agreed to this life of lies that keeps me trapped. I admit we are wealthy now. My "husband" is the District Attorney, we attend every fundraiser and Gala, but our marriage is a sham. We have an agreement that I can have an outside partner since he has one, but our extramarital lovers have signed contracts that say they cannot disclose any details of our dealings. I didn't ask for this, but sometimes you have to make sacrifices to live this life. My self-respect is the only sacrifice I had to make.

Chapter 12

First 48

This is a very sensitive chapter. It can be seen as scary and morbid but I would be doing an injustice if I did not mention this type of wolf. This type of wolf has the hidden qualities of someone whose rage and anger could inevitably take your life.

Personality Traits: Some of these individuals are suffering from mental health issues that may or may not have been diagnosed. Depression, anxiety, bi polar, or even a dominating personality can be seen in this type of wolf. These men either have a dominant personality trait, which can come off as controlling and overwhelming, or they are quiet, passive and seem like they can implode at any time. These guys' moves can vary in the bedroom. They can either engage in rough *50 Shades* sex, or make sweet love to you while listening to Trey Songz.

So what? This man's dominating personality and take charge attitude may be what you like initially. You think to yourself that you have been dating these soft, punk dudes, but you've finally stumbled upon a real man. He is a provider and takes care of your every need. At first, his jealous behavior and constant questioning about your whereabouts seems attractive; he's manly and he cares! How sexy! He has that "bad boy" image with a secret soft side, and you like it! You justify his questioning and always wanting you around as how much he cares about you and is making you a priority. These are lies you tell yourself and your friends to defend what your gut is really saying. Man, let me tell you what happened with my girl Charlene.

WIS Love Story: I am at my friend's birthday dinner on my third glass of Riesling when a fine chocolate man walks in the building. I skim him over quickly enough so that he does not see me checking him out. He is dressed neatly, with a tailored suit, nice watch, and fresh haircut. He's clean cut and classy—just like I like it. He sits at the bar alone and I wonder if he is waiting on someone. A fine man

124

like that cannot possibly be wandering the downtown streets alone. We sing happy birthday and finish our dessert, and I look back at the bar, my sexy stranger is gone. I must admit I was disappointed that I didn't get one more look or at least get to see if he left with someone.

After my friend's birthday dinner, we say, our loud, drunken goodbyes and I go outside to wait for my Uber. As I stand outside scrolling through my Timeline and impatiently tapping my feet, I hear a sexy voice say, "Leaving so soon?" I turn around to see my sexy stranger. I try to act cool, but I know my makeup has worn off, my hair is probably frizzy as hell, and I am so taken aback by his perfectly structured face that all I can mutter is *shole is. Shole is?!?!* I sounded like a country idiot! *What was wrong with me?!* Despite my embarrassment, my Southern drawl amused him. He asked me to join him for a drink inside. I wanted to really bad, but I was nervous and drunk and did not think that I would represent myself well. Before I could come up with some elaborate excuse about needing to walk my dog, my Uber pulled up! Whoo! Saved by the bell! I hopped in and said, "Maybe some other time, Sexy Stranger."

One week later I get a call from the receptionist saying that someone was here to see me. The receptionist also added, "He is so fine girl. So damn fine. Um um um." I come down to the lobby to see Sexy Stranger's fine ass! How in the hell did he find me? Sexy Stranger had a single rose in his hand and when I walked up to him he said, "Is this a good time?" His cologne smelled amazing and that smile was captivating. I fumbled over my words as I told the receptionist to clear all the shit off my calendar. I was gone for the day!

Sexy Stranger, whose name I later found out was Dezmond, was engaging, mysterious, and attentive. He even had a little jealous and protective side that came out when the bartender winked at me. I loved everything I saw about him on that first spontaneous date, and falling head over heels for him was easier than busting your ass after three beers at the ice rink (not that I would know exactly how easy that is). With Dezmond, I felt protected, energized, confident, and sexy. He only had eyes for me and he let me know that I was his.

Things were going so well with Dezmond that I decided to take him to my college's Homecoming weekend celebration. We stayed in a luxurious hotel room overlooking the river and made love at least four times before the tailgating activities. Mind you, the tailgate started at eleven in the morning! Dezmond was a real take charge man in the sheets. He liked to be in control, and even got a little rough sometimes, but I liked it... a lot.

After hours of mind blowing erotica, we *finally* made it to the homecoming festivities. I took Dezmond around all of the tents introducing and showing him off to all of my college classmates. When we got to my fraternity brother's tent, I saw Dezmond's jaw line begin to tense up. *What's up with him* I thought? What does he have against the Alphas? As we made our introductions, one of my Fraternity brothers smugly asked, "Who are you, dog?

Where do we know you from?" "You don't," Dezmond replied with a cold look in his eyes. They stared each other down, and meanwhile Dezmond was squeezing my hand so hard that I thought he was going to break it off. I broke the ice by yelling, "Its Homecoming and time to what??!!!" This got the tent screaming, "Time to partaaaay! And we like to partaaaay!" Dezmond flew out of the tent noticeably angry. He said he was ready to go *now*. We had not even gotten any food yet, and he hadn't met my sorority sisters. Dezmond looked at me with a look so sinister and replied, "I said let's go!" We walked to the car hand in hand, Dezmond clenching mine tightly. I was scared because I had never seen him act this way.

We drove to the hotel in complete silence. I tried to speak, but he held up his finger for me to be quiet. Before the door fully shut to our hotel room, I turned to ask Dezmond what the hell was going on and he slapped the shit out of me. I tasted my blood in my mouth and realized that I was on the floor. Inside, I had a mixture of fear, confusion, and pain. He yelled something but I couldn't hear; I only felt pain and fear. Finally, the yelling stopped, but my face still throbbed. I felt like I was going to pass out because my heart was beating out of my chest. I tried to get up and run, but my body couldn't move and my mind was in such shock that all I could do was sit very still and pray that he went away. He started pacing back and forth, talking to himself in a quick frantic voice. His hands moved back and forth from his head and down to his sides as he paced. Pacing and ranting, ranting and pacing. Finally, he came up to me gently with what looked to be love in his eyes. He said something to me, but I could not hear him. I think he whispered asking me why I made him do that. He began demanding to know why I embarrassed him in front of that guy. Was that my old boyfriend? All of these questions had no answers because I couldn't speak.

He walked away and I heard water running. *What have I gotten myself into? Who is this man? Is he going to kill me?* He came back in what felt like minutes and picked me up; his hands were so warm and gentle. I was confused in every way. *Did this man just lay his hands on me?* I had

129

always thought I would react by whooping some ass, but here I was beaten, bruised, and voiceless. He apologized and bathed me. He was gentle and looked so sincere. He told me that he had too much to drink and lost his temper. He thought that I disrespected him and that he would never lay his hands on me again. He promised me and for some reason I believed him. Maybe it was love. The next week while taking a stroll through Old Towne, he got down on one knee and took out a platinum ring with a heart shaped diamond. He said, "I know I am not perfect, but if you hang in there with me, be my partner, and never give up on me, I will not let you down. I will be the man you always wanted and the man you deserve."

I should have left then. I knew who he was that day I was on the hotel floor. Two broken ribs, one miscarriage, and several black eyes later, I am still here. He doesn't mean it when he loses it, and it's my fault most of the time. He always makes up for it. He needs help, and who am I to leave him when he needs me the most? We are just waiting to locate the right doctor for him. I don't really talk to my friends anymore they are jealous of what we have, so they start hating every time I mention his name. It is just he and I against the world. I know that he will change. I know he gets crazy sometimes, but he doesn't mean to hurt me and always stops before it gets too bad. I know the man I love is in there, and I am committed to helping him figure this out. I'm staying right where I am. He loves me and things will get better. I mean, I am his ride or die.

Caution: These individuals are so emotionally and mentally damaged that they do not think rationally; thus, they don't think their behavior is abnormal. These men call you several times a day checking on your whereabouts, and may accuse you of lying. They believe that women are not trustworthy. Failing or disappointing them could result in a physical or verbal attack. They may display their anger either by being violent, yelling at you, or engaging in tit for tat behaviors. For example, if you stay out all night and crash at a friend's house without calling, they may retaliate by engaging in reckless behavior with another woman just to "teach you a lesson." Or, he may be the type of wolf who has a quiet rage. Though his actions aren't immediate, he is secretly plotting how to hurt you or teach you a big lesson.

This man wants you all to himself, not like the Bottom Feeder who only wants all of your attention and your money; he also wants your heart, soul, time, and attention. This type of wolf wants you 110% of the time, and not only does he not like to share, he actually feels personally disrespected when he has to "share" you with friends, family, or coworkers. You will be able to identify The First 48 because you will feel like you two exist alone on an island. You will have minimal interaction with family and friends, and when they call to check on you, you give responses like, "Everything is fine," "Yes, I am happy," and, "You don't know him like I know him." Women often respond like this out of fear of the level abuse they could be forced to endure by the man that is supposed to love them.

Sher's Suggestions: If you meet an individual and your spidey senses say he is mentally unstable, controlling, too possessive, suicidal, etc... one simple piece of advice, put them on the prayer request list at church and run. Run and do not look back! This type of man is damaged beyond repair by anything less than a miracle working psychiatrist. Every day you stay with him, you are endangering your life. Every day you stay, he is learning your strengths and weaknesses and knows what to say or do to completely control you. If you are a friend to someone like this, you have the hardest job in the world. Women get super defensive about their men, so much so that they shut you out when you are trying to give sound advice. They can perceive you as prying or as a threat to their "happy situation". Sometimes love and good sex can truly make a woman blind to the fact that the man in her life could actually be a threat. If you are a friend and think that your best friend is in this situation, approach gently but ask questions. "Has he hurt you?" "Do you ever feel afraid"? Your friend may get upset with you, but at least you have an idea of how the relationship is really going. Also, try and get as much face time with this individual as possible.

Invite your friend and her possible wolf to dinner and other activities so you can get a good read on their interactions. Lastly, if you think you are overreacting; ask yourself if you would rather that your friend be mad at you or that she ends up seriously injured or even dead. Be diligent, be consistent, and be there for your friend. Your love and support should be unwavering, even if they try and cut you off for side eyeing their man and his First 48 behaviors. You are your sister's keeper.

If you are in an abusive situation with your partner, below are some toll free numbers and resources that you can utilize to get help.

The National Domestic Violence Hotline

1-800-799-SAFE (7233)

http://www.thehotline.org/

Domestic Abuse Intervention Services

http://www.thehotline.org/

1-800-747-4045

Chapter 13

Playbook

If followed correctly this playbook will enable you to:

- Remain logical and not let your emotions speak for you
- Be proactive
- Have the guy chasing you as opposed to it being the other way around

Remaining logical is the best way to prepare you for a successful relationship. Women are known to be irrational, emotional, dramatic, and over react to much of what life throws at us. It is time for a behavior redesign that is very simple to execute.

Fact not fiction- When you find yourself in the middle of a debate, an argument, a complaining session, or even just contemplating a "we need to talk" conversation, remember to stick to the facts as you formulate your response; try to leave your emotions out of it. I know this seems like something you think you already do, but I can assure you that you don't. If you start the conversation with statements such as: *I feel*, *you always*, or *why don't you*, then you have devalued any valid point you were trying to make. Take a look at the situation below and how to handle it.

Problem: Your man does not bring you around his friends.

Why you see this as a problem: His behavior makes you feel like he doesn't want you around him. You may feel like you are a nag, that he enjoys being with his friends without you; it is his own little vacation from you. You assume he is out being a dog and entertaining other chicks when he says he is with his friends. Or, perhaps you have concluded his friends do not like you and he doesn't have the heart to tell you.

Fact: Your man keeps you separate from his friends. He chooses not to allow you to mingle with his pals, even in coed settings.

Old way of handling this situation: A woman should wonder why her man doesn't want her around his friends. Some women may even go to great lengths to try to prove that he is lying about what he is doing OR that he is doing something trifling with his friends. STOP RIGHT THERE! That is the thinking I am talking about. It's ok to have an emotion, but remember to stick to the facts. Women have vivid imaginations and the less communication we get, the more our minds run wild with possibilities. What differentiates us from men is that we come at our man harshly with all of those possibilities as our *proof*. In reality, those possibilities are all in our heads and we owe it to ourselves and our relationships to come to our man calmly, with facts, to discuss the problem.

Behavior redesign: You are more in control of your feelings when you deal with facts. Also, you will get a better response from your man. Instead of him responding to you defensively due to how you came at him, he will be able to listen to you and have a discussion about the situation.

New verbiage:

I've noticed that in the last couple of months you don't include me during gatherings with your friends. I don't understand why I am not invited and it makes me feel (insert feeling here).

Communicating like this gives backing to what you are saying and doesn't make you sound like a raging emotional lunatic. It supports your emotions with facts. If he dares to ask you when he hasn't invited you, give him times, but be sure these are times where,

a) He hasn't asked and you have been available, and

b) You guys were on good terms (no one wants to invite an angry girlfriend or wife to the party).

His response: When you come at him correctly with facts you may get a response like, "Babe, that was not my intention," or "Babe, I didn't realize I did that," or, you may be shocked to hear, "Babe, I didn't think you wanted to be invited." You may also get, "Babe, I hear you, but that is time I spend with friends and no one brings their spouse." Regardless of his response, coming at him with facts and not in an accusatory tone will yield a more truthful response and open a channel that increases positive communication in your relationship.

Next, you want to try and practice proactive behaviors in your relationship.

Proactive Behavior: It allows you to plan what you will say, how you will say it, and what you are expecting as your desired outcome.

The main way to do this is to practice two main behaviors

1) Do not let ill feelings about any situation build up. You may not be ready to talk, but make sure you get your feelings out somehow until the facts are clear

and you can articulate how you feel in a sensible manner.

2) Discuss the uncomfortable and touchy feelings, topics, and ideas with your man when you are both in a good space. The wrong time to bring up these items is during or after an argument, especially if the argument started about something else.

Problem: You use arguments as a time to communicate and unleash all of the ill feelings about your relationship.

How you justify your handling of this problem: You do not see this as a problem. You feel like you are getting this off of your chest or that it just slipped out. You may even tell yourself that you are about to snap on his ass and let him know you feel. After all, he is the one who pushed you to this point.

Old way of handling the situation: In an intense argument about the fact that your man doesn't bring you around his friends, you also choose to mention that you think he has something going on with one of his female friends. You continue by pointing out their communication on social media and how she is always close to him in group pictures as proof of your point.

Behavior redesign: Make a list of all of the things that have been bothering you about your man, your relationship, and how they make you feel. Really dig into each item and determine if these are things you are just tripping about or if they have some serious validity. Once you have narrowed these items down, pick a relaxed time to discuss them with you mate. This should be a time when ya'll are chilling. Do not bring up these items around anyone, right before he is about to embark on something important like a meeting or a presentation, or if one of you will need to leave before you have time to finish the conversation. If you feel like you do not have the time or you simply do not want to converse in person, send him an email and tell him you guys can discuss once you get home.

His response: Your man will appreciate that you didn't add fuel to the fire and bring these items up during an argument. When we are not in our feelings, we are more rational and logical, and taking this approach increases the likelihood that these situations will be discussed in a conversational, instead of argumentative, manner.

The first step in making sure the guy's head over heels about you is checking yourself and your emotion fueled behaviors.

Silence is Golden: In times where the guy has done wrong and you have every right to be upset, or when you have discussed something that he needs to think hard on, the thing to remember is that silence is golden. Silence gives men time to marinate on what you have said or asked. When you come across something of concern in your relationship and you express it, give your mate time to respond. Try not to bombard him with questions and your feelings and sappy emotions. State the facts and how you feel, and wait.

Old way of handling the situation: One important thing to remember is to stay your emotional ass off of social media. I promise this is where we mess up! We write all of our feelings on social media informing everyone that we are in a rough patch with our mate. This does a number of things:

1) It lets other hoes know that he isn't happy with your crazy ass, and

2) It makes you look pathetic and immature. So stop Tweeting, Snapping, Intagraming, and Facebooking while you are down and out about your sig.

Behavior redesign: Do some self-reflection after you have calmly shared your position. In the meantime (because everyone hates waiting for someone else to respond), it may be a good idea to write down some talking points about the situation. *What is the root of the issue? Why did it bother you so much?* Writing and getting your thoughts out are a great form of therapy. Seeing your thoughts on paper can reveal whether you are blowing things out of proportion or if hidden insecurities lie beneath the surface.

If you decide to chat with a close friend about the situation, speak with just one. Sometimes getting counsel from too many friends clouds our judgment because their thoughts infiltrate ours. Remember that your friends are like your hard drive. They remember each man who has hurt you, what they did to hurt you, and how you reacted. Be prepared for your bestie to recant your dating reel highlights, good and bad, and consider them as you make a decision about the status of your current relationship. My advice, however, is vent to your friend (remember *one* friend) and get his/her outlook on the situation, then give yourself quiet time alone to process everything before making a decision about the next steps in your relationship. Ultimately, this responsibility falls back on you, not your gal/guy pal.

Remember ladies, there are plenty of great men out there! Your Newborn may be a keeper; your Dreamer could end up being your future husband! Men often do not come perfectly packaged, but neither are we! Many men are learning, growing, and want to be the best man for you;

they are looking for a quality woman to build a life with. You must ask yourself are you ready to embark in a relationship? Are you willing to improve the ways you perceive yourself and relationships? I would encourage you to be the type of person you want to attract, be patient, enjoy your life and the journey you are on, and be alert for the wolves out there that do not deserve your time, talent, and energies.

Chapter 14

Jackpot

Answers to those hard relationship questions:

Q: Should I sleep with him on the first night?

A: If you decide to give up the goodies on the first night make sure you commit to your decision and will not have regrets no (matter how it plays out). I have slept with a guy on the first night and we ended up in a relationship; I have also slept with a guy on the first night and it ended as a situationship. Behavior is unpredictable and all you can do is make a decision, own up to that decision, and please use protection!

Q: Why are we attracted to wolves anyway?

A: Wolves are sly creatures. These new age men are smart, fine, and successful. The shortage of available men, societal pressures to marry and conceive, loneliness, and sometimes denial about what we want and who we are make us ideal victims for wolves. Now all of the blame is not on them. Resources like this book are meant to develop, enrich and empower women to make better dating decisions and to embrace their true self, flaws and all!

Q: What is your advice on being in a relationship with someone who is co-parenting?

A: Being in a relationship with someone who had a child prior to becoming involved with you is unpredictable—it could be good or bad. Your boyfriend could have a crazy baby mamma. In this case, you <u>DO NOT</u> get into squabbles with a crazy baby mamma; instead your man needs to check her. Or the situation can be easy with a cool baby mamma that has moved on and is only interested in the growth of their child. Regardless of which baby mamma your boyfriend has, your role remains the same. You let the parents make decisions about the child. Make sure that the child respects you. Avoid confrontations with the baby mamma. I know you may feel upset at times that this man already experienced a major life event with another woman, but those are feelings you have to work on if you want to be with him. The circumstance cannot be changed, but you can control the way you react or deal with it.

Q: What do I do if I am dating a mamma's boy?

A: I can't stand dealing with mamma's boys! They run when their mamma comes calling, texting, or demanding that they complete something on the sweetie-do-list. Sometimes the mom doesn't have a man in her life, so she treats her son like her man. He spends money on her, takes her on dates, and has a set appointment every week to spend quality time with her. This cuts into your quality time!

Other times, the mom is over protective and when you come around, she's either disrespectful in the way she speaks to you, or is a mute and just stares at you like a sleazy hussy! Both situations are uncomfortable and annoying. There is nothing wrong with a guy loving on his mom, but sometimes the relationship with his mom can hinder his growing relationship with his mate. My advice is to speak with your man about how his behavior makes you feel—don't flat out call him a mamma's boy, but let him know your true feelings about the situation. Then, let him handle the situation. Hopefully the outcome will be a better balance between his time with his mother and you along with his mom respecting the new lady in his life.

Q: What if I want to keep my man, but the flaws he has are intolerable?

A: Take time to get some business about yourself so you won't be so preoccupied with what a guy is or isn't doing. Come at him correctly regarding the things you feel are intolerable (see chapter 13) and work through his behaviors, how his behaviors make you feel, and how you react to his behaviors. Think rationally and use facts! If you don't see change, it's time to make a tough decision.

Q. If I use all of the techniques you suggest, will this prevent my man from cheating and keep him interested in me?

A. HELL NO!!! Men are men, and <u>each one is different</u>. Often times, men are greedy and them cheating or not being that into you has more to do with them and less to do with you. Your man may be insecure and may cheat because you intimidate him; he may cheat with a lesser woman to feel stronger. Maybe he has a wondering eye because you don't follow the basics from Chapter 1. You have to remain the independent, sexy, and sassy woman he fell in love with. Or, maybe your mate is just a greedy son of a bitch who doesn't know your worth, loves to chase new cat, and doesn't deserve you anyway. Don't fight to make him stay.

Q: I have been with my man for a long time and have seen him fall into a lot of these categories, is that possible?

A. Absolutely! Just as we grow and get to know ourselves, so do men. Our standards have changed from when we were twenty-one, and that will continue. If your standards haven't risen, YOU have the problem, not your man. Some core values will and should stay the same. But, what we want and need out of a relationship will inevitably change, and how we behave and approach love should shift as well.

Q. We have been in a relationship for one year. What should I do to get the ring?

A. Be patient and think some things through. *Why are you considering marrying this man? Are you just ready to get married because "it's time" and everyone else is doing it? Do you really love him and see a future with him? Do you feel like he can lead your household? Has he demonstrated that he can take care of you?* I would think long and hard about these answers and make sure you do not want to get hitched just for a ring and a Facebook post. Once you are real with yourself, you will enjoy the normal pace of the relationship and have more conversations on where it's going. Dating is like an interview; you want to make sure the man is a good fit for you and that you are also a good fit for him. Just because there is a relationship opening does not mean that this person is necessarily qualified for the position. An important thing to remember is you cannot make a man do anything he is not ready to do. All you can do is continue having open conversations about the relationship.

Q. What are some things I should avoid doing if I want him to propose?

A. Definitely do not flirt in his face or disrespect him by still acting very single. A man wants to feel like his prize is unattainable by other men, but if you are flaunting yourself at every club, day party, and on social media, he cannot take you seriously. Also, try and get, and keep your shit together. Maintaining a job, solid work ethic, and good hygiene while fulfilling your role as a constant support system is a great start. Once again, getting down on one knee is totally up to him. Your actions just have to remind him why he would be stupid to allow you to get away.

You cannot get a man to do anything he does not want to and is not ready to do. The only exception to this is if you are holding something over his head. You do not want to have a man that you tricked into being with you (i.e. pregnancy traps, fake illnesses, fulfilling his sexual desires of threesomes even though they make you uncomfortable, or any other situation that is used to manipulate and control).

Q. Should you stay after he has cheated?

A. This really depends on where you are in the relationship, if you want to save the relationship, and why you want to save the relationship. Also, this requires a tough look at yourself. Although his behavior was wrong, did you push him into another woman's arms by not being a good partner? Did you turn into a prude that only likes missionary with the lights off? Did you fail to check yourself before flying off the handle one too many times about some chick that liked his posts on Instagram? You have to determine if you could have played a role in his infidelity, and if you did, you have to own it. Above all, decide if you want to forgive him and what that will look like. If you are going to bring up his cheating every week or have sex with a guy you pull off your friend zone bench as retaliation, then you might as well end the relationship.

Q: Should you cheat?

A: No, if you feel like you want to cheat because of a need for retaliation, you are bored, or your ex is still slinging some serious vitamin D, then you are not ready to be in a committed relationship anyway. Now I know some women cheat to fill a void, but sleeping with another man is a short term solution that will end badly. You can only get away with sleeping around for so long before you get caught, and every time you open your legs for your side boo, you are increasing the likelihood of getting caught and jeopardizing everything you have built with your mate. The universe works in mysterious ways, and you always want to set yourself up to receive blessings.

Q: What are the deal breakers?

A: Cheating, abuse (physical, verbal, psychological, emotional), disrespect of you or your loved ones, neglect, stealing from you or your family, and constant lying about anything. You are too good of a woman to have to tolerate any of these. Get out now!

Q: He doesn't call me his girlfriend but we have been talking for some months. Should I keep waiting?

A: You should bring this topic up one time, and if he gives you some bull shit answer (see Chapter 5), and then drop his ass. Right now you are in a situationship, and if a relationship is what you truly desire, you are going to have to find it elsewhere with someone ready to give it to you.

Q: Should we have open dialogue about our past relationships?

A: I would keep this to a minimum (See Chapters 2 and 7).

Q: The man I'm dating is in the process of getting a divorce. Should I continue the relationship or wait until its final?

A: Wait until it's over. I know you think you are a big girl and can handle it, but until the divorce is final, this man is still married, and he may decide to return to his wife (and kids if they have any). If you have a thing for messing with married men, you need more help than this book can offer.

Q: How can I tell if my boyfriend is controlling?

A: A controlling boyfriend asks every detail about your whereabouts before, during, and after you leave the house (and that is if he allows you to leave the house at all). He texts you constantly and always wants you to be in constant sight. He may also control what you eat by ordering for you or dismissing the things you say you want. He doesn't like your friends and probably suggests that you do not speak with family either.

Q: How do I get him to chase me again?

A: Make sure that you are confident and you look and feel beautiful on the inside and out (Please note that beauty standards vary from person to person, so you have to be the judge of how your beauty makes you feel). Keep an agenda of activities that do not include him and make sure to get out of pocket sometimes. Be unpredictable, spontaneous, and adventurous. (See Chapters 1 & 13)

Q: Am I in a toxic relationship?

A: Usually in a toxic relationship, you feel unhappy, lower than low, antisocial, and other areas of your life begin to deteriorate as a result. The frequent arguing, name calling, and lack of interest and support from your mate begins to pollute other areas of your life. You may begin to put on weight, call out of work frequently, avoid speaking to friends, or even begin drinking more. Your physical and mental reaction to your relationship will let you know if this is a healthy relationship that challenges you or if it weighs you down and keeps you down.

Q: Things aren't the same as in the beginning. Is he losing interest in me?

A: Not necessarily. Your man could be trying to deal with pressure at work, maybe something is bothering him and he does not know how to communicate, or perhaps your relationship does need a spark (See chapter 1)! However, if he would rather be anywhere but with you, does not return your calls or texts, does not initiate calling you, and has every excuse as to why he can't give you quality time, then yes—he is probably losing interest.

Q: How are they so happy with someone else and why didn't I get all the special treatment? Was I not good enough?

A: Good question! His new happiness has more to do with him and less to do with you. People bring out different things in each other, and maybe your relationship did not bring out those types of things. I would not burden yourself with why because what you *see* may not always be an accurate depiction of the truth. The point is that he has moved on and you should try and do the same in a healthy way.

Q: Will I ever trust again?

A: This is totally up to you. Please don't make the same mistake I made in previous relationships. Take your time to love yourself again, invest time in family and friends who love and support you, and move slowly. Celebrate victories and be open to discussing insecurities and vulnerabilities with a trusted friend. That will help build your trust from the inside. It starts with trusting yourself.

Q: How do I start the process of healing after a breakup?

A: First remove your ex-partner from social media. I know you want to be nosy and see what they are doing, but you need a break from them holding a place in your life. Do not express your feelings about the break up over social media! Next, you want to do things that make you happy and commit to learning (or at least trying) something new.

Journaling helps as well because you can get your feelings out in a private way. Also, prayer and time are the two essentials that you need to get over someone you love. I know some of you are saying that sleeping with someone new is the best way to heal after a breakup, but this will only complicate your feelings and can lead you down a path you are not ready to go down. If you are horny and missing that constant Vitamin D supply, visit your nearest sex toy store. This method is safer and you will not feel like shit once you have reached your climax.

Q: Should I cease all communication after a breakup?

A: Yes, it's called a break up for a reason. You are not ready to be friends, and the constant communication only perpetuates your desire for them to be in your life. Stay strong! Block his number!

Q: Why do guys chase you then act uninterested when they get you?

A: Guys love the chase, and when we allow them to catch up to us, they start acting comfortable. You always want to keep a guy guessing until you all are in a committed relationship. Do not let him know he is the only guy with your attention while dating. Make it seem like winning you is a prize; they need to make their best effort to win your time, love, and energies. Let the Lover Games Begin!

Q: Is it ok for my guy to still communicate with his ex?

A: Not unless they have a child together and these conversations need to be about co-parenting. His ex is not your friend (in some rare cases she can be your friend), and doesn't owe you any respect or loyalty, so in a weak moment, a conversation with his ex may become a quickie. She will have no remorse because he was hers first, and you can only be so surprised if you have been supporting their "friendship" all along.

Q: Why won't he put pictures of us on social media?

A: Nowadays, the realness of our entire lives is proven or disproven on social media. We live in a world where if we do not post about something, it isn't real. Your guy is either not wanting to draw attention to the relationship (maybe attention from past relationships), or perhaps he is private and does not want everyone in his business. Whatever the reason, make sure you ask him about it using the guidelines from Chapter 13.

Q: I met a great guy with no car and in between jobs. Am I a gold digger if I stop dating him?

A: Even if you are a gold digger, there are just some basics every guy should have. You are the prize and should be treated as such, but this is difficult when you are always footing the bill or using your gas to scoop him up. This gets old after a while and you want to make sure that both parties are contributing their fair share of time, finances, and love to the relationship. This is the only way the relationship has a chance of surviving.

Q: If the guy is a great guy and the sex is bad, should I stay?

A: Bad sex does not mean that he will not want to have sex, so regardless, you will still have to put out and not enjoy it every time. Are you willing to do that? Determine why you feel as though he has bad sex. Is it the size, his technique, or lack of experience? If his bad sex is the result of the latter two, then show him what you like in a cool, sexy, and fun way. This problem may be able to be remedied. If his penis is non-existent and he has bad technique, you may want to leave before you end up cheating with someone that can really fulfill your sexual needs.

Q: What are the ways to a man's heart?

A: TLC had the answer to this! You want to be crazy, sexy, and cool. When I say *crazy*, I do not mean extra jealous and territorial. I mean spontaneous, fun, and open minded. You want to keep your *sexy* instead of getting comfortable just because you have a man. Lastly, you want to be *cool* enough to hang with the guys. This may require you to learn a thing or two about sports, cooking, hosting, and hanging out with his friends. Additionally, being honest and sticking to the facts (See Chapter 13), showing compassion, and being supportive are also the ways to a man's heart.

Q: If a man knows he does not want to be with a woman for the long run, why still date her/be with her instead of letting her go?

A: A man in this situation is getting exactly what he wants; whether it be guaranteed sex, arm candy, or a warm body to fill his lonely void. Each chapter in this book gives you some red flags to be able to identify and avoid wolves like this.

Q: What is the true definition of dating?

A: These days dating or "talking" is when you are seeing someone regularly. You may have slept together, and you like to spend time with them, but he may not be the only guy getting your time and you may not be the only girl on his call log.

Q: How can you be more intimate with your partner outside of the bedroom?

A: Great question! Intimacy is so much more than switching from doggy style to cowgirl so you can stare in his eyes. In fact, you can be intimate with long, deep talks about life, love and your future without any physical interactions. You can also be intimate with foot rubs, long hot baths or showers, or even watching the sunset. Any moment that is special and between just you two, whether it be conversation, affection, or the creation of a special memory, can build intimacy.

References

Kassoy, B. (2014, January 24). 8 Reasons most guys actually hate strip clubs. *Glamour Magazine: Smitten.* Retrieved from http://www.glamour.com/sex-love-life/blogs/smitten/2014/01/what-guys-think-8-reasons-i-ha.